AF553864

Management of Teacher Education

Management of Teacher Education

B.C. Das

A.P.H. PUBLISHING CORPORATION
4435-36/7, ANSARI ROAD, DARYA GANJ
NEW DELHI-110 002

Published by
S.B. Nangia
A.P.H. Publishing Corporation
4435–36/7, Ansari Road, Darya Ganj,
New Delhi-110002
Phone: 011–23274050
e-mail: aphbooks@gmail.com

2026

Rs.1495/-

Typeset by
Ideal Publishing Solutions
C-90, J.D. Cambridge School,
West Vinod Nagar, Delhi-110092

Printed at
RD DIGITAL PRINTERS
Ansari road , Daryaganj, Delhi-110002

This book is based, with a little deviation, on the report of a project exclusively supported and financed by the University Grants Commission (UGC) New Delhi. However, the facts and views expressed herein and the conclusions drawn are entirely that of the author and not of the UGC.

PREFACE

Teacher training at the tertiary level is not a new concept to the countries like the USA, Russia, the UK, Papua New Guinea, Manitoba, Queens land, Sweden, Australia, Canada, Singapore, Malaysia, China, and Korea. In 1982, UNESCO regional office, Bangkok, brought out a document compiling the case studies of teacher training programmes for university and college teachers in Asia. In India academic staff development of the university system was emphasized as long ago as the mid sixties. Even when the Fourth Plan was being drawn, the Task Force on Higher Education appointed by the Planning Commission mooted this idea. Something was done in consequence of this initiative. Over the years, teacher fellowships and similar programmes were launched, but nothing like a system got evolved. During 1987, a number of Academic Staff Colleges ASCs) were established. Thus, beginning as an experiment ASCs have made a steady progress in India by offering induction programmes, orientation programmes, refresher courses and short term courses to a large number of teachers, administrators, educationists, etc. who are directly associated with higher education in various ways. The success of these courses during this period was weighed in terms of the personnel trained. However, an aspect of far more serious concern than quantity is the quality and academic credibility of these courses. It is unfortunate that no serious efforts were made *to* consolidate and qualitatively uplift the teachers' retraining during this period.

The present volume is a research project in the area of orientation of university and college teachers which was funded by the UGC and was concerned with exploration and critical evaluation of the systems adopted for the management of teaching and learning in the existing ASCs in India. Having selected a 25% sample of the existing ASCs, the practices, procedures and strategies adopted by them for the management of various sub-systems of the system of teaching and learning have been surveyed. The sub-systems specifically studied were: (a) Selection of Participants, (b) Course Content and Course Materials, (c) Organisation, Administration and Duration, (d) Co-curricular and Financial Aspects of the programmes,

(e) Resource Persons, (f) Methodology, (g) Evaluation, (h) Problems and (i) Future Plans. The survey systems adopted for the management of teaching and learning in the existing ASCs were critically evaluated against the opinions and reactions of 765 teachers, selected randomly from the institutions included in the sample, about the suitability and efficiency of the system adopted.

In this report, while the Introductory Chapter traces the development of teacher education in India in historical perspective and prepares the case for under taking this study. The Chapter 2 presents the 'Method and Procedures' adopted for conducting the study. The remaining ten Chapters discuss, in detail, the results of the survey, evaluation of each sub-system in synthesized form and the problems faced by the ASCs in organizing Orientation Programmes (OPs) and their Future Plans for improvement. Specifically, Chapter 3 'Selection of Participants' presents the result and evaluation pertaining to the process and procedure adopted for the intake, selection, catchment areas, sufficiency of the participants, repeated admission to the OPs and format evolved for the establishment of the ASCs. The Chapter 4 evaluates the 'Course Content and Course Materials' in the light of planning and executing, structuring, preparing, suitability and quality of the Course Content and Course Materials, and purposes and academic values of OPs. The Chapter 5 'Orientation, Administration and Duration of Course' deals with the number of OPs organized by the ASCs in one year, Compulsory/Voluntary participation in OPs, suitability of the OPs, Core Staff, Standing Committee, infrastructures, suitability of duration of the OPs, daily working hours for teachers, suitability of time devoted to lecture/discussion and practicals. The Chapter 6 'Co-curricular and Financial Aspects of the OP' evaluates the on the campus and off the campus activities and the financial aspects of the OPs. The Chapter 7 'Resource Persons' presents a discussion about the selection criteria of resource persons, cooperation from and identification and suitability of resource persons in terms of course content, knowledge, presentation and as a teacher as perceived by the participants. The Chapter 8 'The Methodology followed in OPs', evaluates the methods adopted for delivering course content, suitability of and satisfaction with the methodology, selection and suitability of teaching media and aids used, mode and suitability of interactions offered to the participants, and above all the feedback on delivering lecture and individual interaction. The Chapter 9 'The Evaluation' takes a critical stock of practices adopted for the formative and summative evaluation of teacher participants' performance. The Chapter 10 'Problems of the ASCs' deals with the problems in relation to Core Staffs, participations, resource persons, course content, methodology, reading materials, infrastructure, and finance for organizing OPs. Chapter 11 'Future Plans' discusses the plans and programmes that the ASCs in India have proposed for their development in the future. The last Chapter 12 'Findings and Suggestions' presents the major findings of the study and suggests adequate measures for the improvement of the OPs offered by the ASCs in India. In presenting the results of the survey and analysis of teacher participants' opinions and reactions, an attempt has been made in each Chapter to critically reflect upon each sub-system and draw implications and suggestions for improvements.

Although the National Level Project on which the present book is based, yet keeping in mind the recommendation of the Mehrotra Committee (1986) for launching staff development programmes through distance education methodology, the last chapter, being a deviation from the project, was devoted to offer a non-traditional possibility for organising teacher education programmes through distance education.

I shall fail in my duty if I do not put on record the contributions of all those by whose encouragements and efforts the study could be completed and the report has come out in its present form. First of all, I wish to thank the University Grants Commission (UGC), New Delhi for financing this project. My special thanks go to Mr. Lekhan Gogoi who worked as the Project Fellow and was on his toes for the supplication of the study. Mr. Bablu Mahanta and Mr. Amit Paul deserve special thanks as they took all pains to bring out the report in the present format. The cooperations and encouragements received from friends and well wishers were throughout appreciable and deserve acknowledgement. In the end, I wish to put on record the help, cooperation and encouragements that I received from my wife, Pranati, and sons Biplab and Parth.

North Eastern Hill University **B.C. Das**
Tura, Meghalaya

Foreword

It is a great pleasure for me to write the 'Foreword' for this book which is the culmination of a research project funded by the UGC and deals with very burning problem of impact evaluation of teaching, training and learning in the existing Academic Staff Colleges. Various problems faced by the Academic Staff Colleges towards successful running of orientation courses have been identified. Twenty five percentage of the existing Academic Staff Colleges have been selected randomly and nine parameters based on the identified problems have been studied including selection of participants, course contents and course material, resource persons, methodology, evaluation, problems and future plans.

The author has given many suggestions for improvement. Some of them are (i) Adequate co-ordination between college participants and Academic Staff College, (ii) More emphasis on teaching techniques, (iii) Identifying problems faced by participants in their class rooms, (iv) Regular feedback from the participants and modifying the programme accordingly, (v) Practical approach to teaching, (vi) Careful choice of resource persons from Universities, Industries, Bank, Government Organization, NGO's etc., (vii) Inclusion of component of professional ethics of teachers, educational technologies, problem of youth etc. in staff development programmes, (viii) Development of monitoring system to examine the impact of programmes and scope of improvement (ix) More frequency of orientation programmes and (x) Less number of participants (maximum 30) to encourage interactive and participatory teaching instead of traditional class room teaching.

The author has also emphasized the role of distance education for teacher training. Looking at the huge number of teacher participants needing updation regularly and also from economic point of view, the author is of the considered opinion that staff—development programme through the distance education will be more viable and effective.

I am confident that the findings made through this project and various suggestions made in this book will go a long way towards the improvement of teacher training programmes at the tertiary level and qualitative uplift of academic standards of teacher participants through orientation programmes, refresher courses and short term courses conducted by Academic Staff Colleges which in turn will contribute significantly towards the improvement of class room teaching in particular and college and university education in general.

S.S. KHARE
Pro-Vice- Chancellor
North Eastern Hill University
Tura Campus
Chandmari - 794002, Tura

Contents

CHAPTER-I

INTRODUCTION

In this Chapter we will, first, trace the historical development of teacher education starting from the professional training of Primary School Teachers to the professional orientation and in-service training of College and University Teachers in India. We will then explain the status, importance and responsibility of the teacher in higher education. Thereafter, we will describe the meaning and importance of the Academic Staff Colleges, and trace its genesis. Then we will highlight its functions, and state the objectives and need of the Orientation Programme with research supports. After this, we will present the Academic Staff College Scheme evolved by the University Grants Commission. Then we will describe the need for the study followed by its objectives and significance. We will conclude the chapter by presenting the delimitations of the study.

GROWTH OF TEACHER EDUCATION IN INDIA

Professional education of teachers in India has not been a static but an evolutionary process. The system has grown gradually starting with the establishment of the first Normal School for the professional education of primary school teachers in 1793 to the establishment of hundreds of training colleges and university departments of education for the professional training of secondary school teachers. The need for the professional orientation and in-service education of university and college teachers in India, till recently, has not, however, been felt as strongly as it has been felt for the school level teachers. Two causes seem to be responsible for this in attention towards the professional orientation of tertiary level teachers: the first can be attributed to historical reasons; and the second lies in the general feeling of the university academics that such an orientation is not required at this level, as they often argue that successful and stalwart teachers exist in universities and they never received any formal orientation in pedagogy and teaching. The historical reasons are examined in the followings sections.

Historically, in the pre-independent India the British wanted to propagate English culture through their western system of education. They wanted to generate an army of Indians who were black in hair and dark in complexion but English in taste and appreciation, so as to render low cadre white-collar jobs in their reign. Thus, they geared their system of education to achieve this aim focused mainly on the school education. It is for this reason that one finds that almost all the committees and commissions appointed in pre-independent India were concerned with school education. They wanted to impart effective western education in their schools and to this effect they realised the need and importance of professional training of school teachers. This is clearly reflected in the reports of the committees and commissions instituted by them from time to time to gear educational system to achieve their set aims.

For example, Wood's Despatch, 1854, resulted in the establishment of Normal Schools for primary level school teachers. The Wood's Despatch, however states that:

> *"Our present aim should be to improve the teachers whom we find in possession. They should be encouraged to attend the normal schools and classes, which may thereafter be instituted for this class of teachers. We desire to see the establishment with as little day as possible of training schools and classes for masters in each presidency of India."*

Thereafter, the Indian Education Commission, 1882, recommended that:

> *"An examination in the principles and practice of teaching be instituted, success in which should thereafter be a condition of permanent employment as a teacher in any secondary school, Government or aided and graduates willing to attend a course of*

instruction in a normal school in the principles and practice of teaching be required to undergo a shorter course of training than others" (Report of the Indian Education Commission, 1882-83, p. 259).

However, the two Government of India resolutions 1904 and 1913, besides recognising the need of pre-service orientation and training of school teachers, emphasized the importance and hence the need for in-service education of these teachers. For example, the 1904 resolution categorically recommended that:

"It is necessary for a training college to maintain a close relation with the school, so that the student on leaving the college and entering upon his career as a teacher may not neglect to practice the methods which he was taught. The old students of a training college should be occasionally brought together again and that the inspecting staff should cooperate with college authorities in seeing that the influence of the college makes itself felt in the school" (Government of India, Education Policy, 1904).

Almost similar were the contents of the 1913 resolution. For instance, the resolution stated that:

"The trained students whom the college has sent out should be occasionally brought together again and the inspecting staff should cooperate with the training college authority in seeing that influence of the college makes itself felt in the schools. As teachers left to themselves are liable to deteriorate, there are great advantages in the periodical repetition and improved courses during school vacation."

Thus, while the two resolutions visualized the cooperating role of the training colleges for the in-service education and reorientation of school teachers; the Hartog Committee, appointed in 1929, went a step ahead in recognising the need of the in-service reorientation of school teachers and suggested a different strategy. The report in this regard stated that:

> *"Even under ideal condition where the right type of teachers have been selected and well trained, the teacher is much isolated and must often be in need of guidance and encouragement. Journals, refresher courses, conferences and meetings can do much to brighten the lives of the teachers and improve their work" (Hartog Committee's Report, 1929, pp. 81-82).*

As a consequence of the recommendations of the Hartog Committee, there was a sporadic organisation of refresher courses in the states of Uttar Pradesh and Madras. But these courses could not become a permanent feature for want of adequate finances. However, the Abbott and Wood Report, 1937 can be considered a significant attempt in the history of professional orientation of teachers in the sense that it, for the first time, saw pre-service training of school teachers as distinctly separate from the in service training. Not only this, it for the first time, paved the way for the establishment of regular programmes for the in-service reorientation of school teachers. For example, the report stated that:

> *"We are of the opinion that the training of teachers should consist of two distinct parts. First, a pre-employment training of students in normal schools and later refresher courses for practising teachers. If the spirit of those who have had something before entering upon their work is to be kept alive and if their technical skill as teachers is to be improved; it is vital that they should have opportunities from time to time to attend Refresher Courses" (Abbott Wood Report, 1937, pp. 24-25).*

Keeping in view the financial and manpower difficulties faced by the country at that time, Abbott and Wood realised the constraints in the way of implementing their two-fold training programmes for the teacher throughout the country. Thus, they suggested the following implementing strategy:

> *"The time may not yet be ripe for the logical outcome of this concept of the two-fold nature of training of teachers. But in course of time there aught to be in each province a Government Training College*

> *comfortably housed, well equipped and organized and staffed for the purpose of providing a sequence of refresher courses of one or two months duration throughout the year" (Abbott and Wood Report, 1937, pp. 26-27).*

Again, in 1944, the Central Advisory Board of Education presented a scheme of education, popularly known as the 'Sargent Scheme', based on the report presented by John Sargent, the then secretary of education. The report proposed a plan of educational reconstruction giving special note for an improved organisation of teacher preparation. Regarding the in-service training of teachers, the report suggested:

> *"In addition to the provision for the actual training of teachers, refresher courses... be provided at frequent intervals in order to keep trained teachers up to date. Such courses should cover all the subjects of the curriculum as well as ideas and methods of general interest. They are of the greatest importance in a country where a large number of teachers necessarily serve in isolated villages" (The Sargent Report, 1944, p. 64).*

This brief historical review of the development regarding the professional orientation of teachers during the pre-independence period substantiates the hypothesis that the focus of the British educational policy was upon the quality of teaching and teachers at the school level. The university and college education though saw a modest development during their reign but the need for professional orientation and in-service education of university and college teachers was neither felt nor recognized in the pre-independent India.

Probably because of this neglect by the aliens and because of the recognition of the role that higher education could play in the national development, our national leaders exhibited their foresightedness by appointing the University Education Commission soon after independence in 1949 under the chairmanship of Dr. S. Radha Krishnan. Although the recommendations of the

University Education Commission were very innovative and roots of many of the practices of higher education even today can be attributed to it. Yet, it is quite surprising that the commission remained silent about the professional orientation of the university and college teachers. Though it recognized the weaknesses of the teaching system and showed concern about large number of failures in the under graduate courses, but it did not attribute these weaknesses and wastage to the quality of teachers in the universities and colleges. Rather the commission seemed to be convinced that the main cause behind this wastage was the supply of poor, ill-equipped students from the schools and intermediate colleges to the universities. It is probably this conviction that led the commission to recommend "Refresher Courses for High School and Intermediate College Teachers." The Commission recommended that:

> *"An urgent reform is the institution of vacation refresher courses for high school and intermediate college teachers ...we believe that vacation courses should best be organized by the universities and that they should form the chief feature of the Extension Programme of each University. Our Universities have not realized that they owe a responsibility towards those high schools, and intermediate colleges from which they draw their students. What could be more appropriate than to organize refresher courses for teachers who need to and should be encouraged to extend, refurnish and up to date their knowledge" (The Report of the University Education Commission, 1949, p. 95).*

The University Education Commission justified the need for organizing refresher courses for the High School and Intermediate College teachers by the universities on the following grounds:

> *"It is extra-ordinary that our school teachers learn all of whatever subject they teach before reaching the age of twenty-four or twenty-five and then all their further education is left to 'experience', which in most cases is another name for stagnation. We must realize that*

> *experience needs to be supplemented by experiment before reaching its fullness, and that teacher, to keep alive and fresh, should become a learner from time to time. Constant outpouring needs constant in taking; practice must be reinforced by theory, and the old must be constantly tested by the new."(Pp. 95-96).*

The Commission also recommended that the scheme of refresher courses could be made a real success if the authorities of schools and colleges and the Government Education Departments made certified attendance a university refresher-course once every four or five years, a qualification for promotion.

Are these observations not true to justify the professional orientation of teachers teaching in the universities and colleges through refresher or other types of courses? Do the university and college teachers not need to up-date knowledge to keep pace with the fast growth of knowledge? Do they not need to keep alive and fresh to render best possible in most effective way to the younger generation? The answers to all these questiors is yes. The University Education Commission did not accept this as a need, probably because most of the members of this commission were stalwart teachers and they had never received any formal professional orientation or training in pedagogy of teaching.

The First Conference of the Principals of Training Colleges was held at Baroda in 1950. The Conference recommended, "To ensure the continued professional growth of trained teachers and to prevent their lapse into unprogressive methods, refresher course both general and special should be organized". The conference also recommended shorter course for untrained teachers working in class, refresher course for trained teachers and special courses for those teachers who wanted to have any advanced training in a specific field.

In 1953, the Secondary Education Commission observed that:

> *"However excellent the programme of teacher training may be it does not itself produce an excellent teacher ... increased efficiency will come through experience, practically analyzed and through new and group*

> *efforts at improvement. The teacher training institution should accept its responsibility for assisting the in-service stage of teacher training. Among the activities, which the training college should serve or in which it should collaborate, are:*

(i) Refresher Courses,

(ii) Through Intensive Courses in Special Subjects,

(iii) Practical Training in Workshop,

(iv) Seminars and Professional Conferences.

"It should also allow its staffs to serve as consultants to school or group of schools conducting some programmes of improvement."

It was only in 1966, the Education Commission often referred to as Kothari Commission recognized the need for the reorientation of the university and college teachers for the first time in India. In this regard the commission stated that:

"An important point of emphasis would be the reorientation of the university teachers to adopt new and improved techniques of teaching and evaluation. A programme of seminars, discussions or workshops should be organized to serve as the spearhead of the reform"(Report of the Education Commission, 1964-66, p. 526). The commission in this regard further hinted the content of the courses and pointed out mode of delivery of the suggested content as below:

> *"Every university and college should have regular orientation courses organized for a few weeks early in the session in which some new and some older teachers participate. The best teachers of the institution as well as some distinguished teachers from outside should discuss with them the outstanding problems of teaching, research, and discipline, as well as the mechanics of the profession (p. 155).*

In order to achieve this and ensure the success of the suggestions made, the commission recommended the following strategy for implementing the scheme for the professional reorientation of the university and college teachers:

> *"It may be possible in bigger universities on a permanent and continuing basis by establishing something like a staff college, where teachers from all affiliated and constituent colleges as well as the university will be brought together for orientation, discussions, seminars, workshops, etc. Where this is not possible, a conference centre would he necessary to facilitate discussion of the subject matter, etc. The Staff College of the Conference Centre should also produce, in cooperation with other members of the faculty, occasional brochures, book lists, guidance materials, etc., of use to all teachers" (Report of the Education Commission, 1964-66, p. 156).*

Thus, it is seen that the Education Commission, 1964-66, not only recognized the need for professional reorientation of university teachers but also for the first time mooted the idea of establishing Staff Colleges in leading universities. The staff colleges were conceived to serve as permanent places for organizing reorientation courses for freshly appointed university teachers on a regular basis; and serve as forums for professional updating of the university faculty by launching refresher courses. Although the recommendation of the Kothari Commission regarding the professional orientation of university teachers received the attention of some universities and a few orientation programmes had been started by them immediately after the report was submitted in 1966. But for reasons difficult to list, the scheme of launching staff colleges for the professional reorientation of the university teachers remained dormant for almost two decades.

However, as an impact of these recommendations the need for the professional orientation of the university teachers was felt and recognized in some parts of the country. A number of seminars and conferences were organized in the early seventies, the significant among them were those held at the M.S. University, Baroda; Meerut University, Meerut; University of Bombay, etc. These conferences not only generated a consensus about the urgent need of courses for the professional reorientation of the university teachers but also a few courses were chalked out, e.g.

"Programme for University Teachers, M.S. University, Baroda"(Yadav and Roy, 1977). Further, in response to the felt need of having professional orientation courses for the university teachers, a few enthusiastic universities during the mid seventies " started regular orientation programmes for teachers, e.g. Diploma in Higher Education (Bombay), Master of College Teaching (Calicut), Diploma in Education (Madras)". This brief historical review of the development pertaining to the professional training and orientation of teachers in India since 1854, reveals that the professional training and in-service reorientation of school teachers received a recurring attention of the various expert committees and commissions appointed from time to time; and this led to gradual development of systematic pre-service and in-service training programmes for the school teachers. However, in the case of professional orientation of university and college teachers it was only after the recommendation of the Education Commission -1966 that the need for such a course began to be reorganized and some debate on this issue was generated in the country. Though a few universities launched regular programmes for the professional orientation of university teachers, but these were sporadic in nature and quite divergent in aims. Though divergent in aims, such efforts were the pioneering beginnings in the professional preparation of university teachers and proved to be a stepping-stone for the professional preparation and reorientation of university teachers on an ongoing basis in the near future.

The National Policy on Education - 1986, with regard to the teacher education states that:

> *"Teacher education is a continuous process, and its pre-service and in-service components are inseparable. At the first step, the system of teacher education will be overhauled. District Institute of Education and Training (DIET) will be established with the capability to organize pre-service and in-service courses for elementary school teachers for the personnel working in non-formal and adult education. As DIETs get established, sub-standard institutions will be phased out. Selected Secondary Teacher*

Training Colleges will be upgraded to complement the work of State Councils of Educational Research and Training. The National Council of Teacher Education will be provided the necessary resources and capability to accredit institutions of teacher education and provide guidance regarding curricula and methods. Networking arrangements will be created between institutions of teacher education and university departments of education " (NPE, 1986 p. 26). The Policy not only recognized the importance of training of elementary and secondary school teachers as stated above but also recommended the training or orientation of university and college teachers in the beginning of the service as well as continuing education thereafter.

TEACHERS IN HIGHER EDUCATION

Higher education implies more specialized study normally undertaken after successful completion of a good basic education, which normally lasts for 11 years. The term 'Higher Education' signifies higher courses in any institution. Under this comes education in Colleges, Universities and Centres of Advanced Studies. The colleges include both graduate and postgraduate colleges affiliated to the universities getting grant-in-aid or controlled and managed by State Governments. Universities are famous for their quality and standard and pursue research work of a very high order. They can be classified according to their constitution in three categories- affiliating, unitary and federal.

Higher education should ultimately aim at search for truth and achievement of excellence. It must promote the development of total personality of students and inculcate in them the commitment to society. It has been realised that higher education is not a means of awarding degrees and distribution of favours, it is a means of improving the quality of life of everybody, to live with dignity in a highly competitive world.

By the end of 1970s, the pyramidal structure of education has changed in developed and developing countries compared to what it had been two decades earlier. The United States and Canada have now graduated from the stage of mass education to that of universal access to secondary and higher education. Developed countries outside Europe and North America, such as Japan, Australia and New Zealand have greatly advanced their rate of students completing secondary and higher education. Even the developing countries like India and Pakistan have taken tremendous efforts to broaden their educational opportunities.

India has a long tradition of learning. There were gurukulas' and ashrams' run by individual scholars in ancient times. There also existed parishads or assemblies of renowned scholars, where disputable points in connection with religion were discussed. During the Buddhist period, a number of viharas and sangharams or monasteries' developed into a kind of educational centres. The Universities of Purushapura, Takshashila, Jagaddal, Vikramashila and Odantpuri, Nalanda, Jayendra Vihara, Kanchi, Vallabhi and other centers were some of the famous places. The Muslims established their own institutions of higher learning in Delhi, Agra, Lucknow, Jaipur, and several other places.

The development of higher education during modern period can be divided into:

The age of colleges (from the early days of the British rule till 1857)

The era of parent universities (1957 to 1917)

The rise of new universities (1917 to 1947)

And higher education in Post - Independence period.

The number of university level institutions during the last decades have increased from 19 to 425, of colleges from about 700 to 20,000 and of students from 0.2 to 12 million. Though the numbers of Colleges and Universities have increased by leaps and bounds, it is felt that the quantitative expansion has not been accompanied by qualitative improvement. The system is compared to radar less ship on the high seas. The huge machine consumes a tremendous amount of national energy, finance, time, physical resources and investments in man and material, but yields output of quality and utility.

The draft proposal on higher education for the 21st century adopted in the UNESCO World Conference on Higher Education (1998) envisages the quality of higher education as a multidimensional concept. It has been realised that the quality depends on:

(i) Quality of content and techniques of education

(ii) Quality of the infrastructure

(iii) Quality of students and

(iv) Quality of teacher

An individual of high teaching skill and competence may be appointed as a teacher but one cannot force him to apply his knowledge and skill unless he is motivated to do so. The success of an educational system depends to an extent on the teaching methodology, competence and motivation of the teacher himself who is at the centre of the stage. He should be committed to his subject and develop the same commitment in his students. As the backbone of the educational system and architect of society, it is the responsibility of the teacher to guide and inspire his students and enrich his discipline.

The dream of a learning society can become a reality only when the teachers are well equipped with moral, professional, intellectual, practical and communication skills to convince the customers through their efficient service.

The status of the teacher reflects the socio-cultural ethos of a society. The importance of teacher in higher education has been dealt in detail by University Education Commission (1949). The commission is of the view that the success of an educational process depends on the character and ability of the teacher. Butler (1950) describing the position and role of teacher from the idealistic point of view says that the "Teacher is central in this pattern of Education". The teacher has a vital role to play in our effort to relate education to national development and social change. It is the responsibility of the teacher to guide and inspire his students, to enrich his discipline, to inculcate values, which are in consonance with other cultural heritage and social objectives. This involves the transmission of knowledge from one generation to the other and extension of the boundaries of knowledge through research, investigation and enquiry. In its most comprehensive sense, teaching includes behaviour of teachers that are intended to cause student learning. His success will be measured not in terms of percentage of passes alone but through the quality of life and character of men and women of the society whom he has taught.

Henry Rosovsky, Dean of the Faculty of Arts and Science at Harvard University says "At Harvard we ask a traditional question: who is the most qualified person in the world to fill a particular vacancy. Then we try to persuade that scholar to join our ranks. We may not succeed in attracting our first or even our second choice, but our goal is elevated". It has been realised that, after independence, as the higher education system expanded and additional teaching posts were created, the principle of recruiting the most qualified person in the country to each teaching post was gradually compromised. The target group for search successively shrank because of regional and communal considerations. It is again said that if one were to single out the factor most responsible for the gradual decline in the academic standards in higher education, it can be said without hesitation that it was because teaching posts were invariably not filled by recruiting the best qualified persons. Therefore, it is believed that the most important task for a Vice-Chancellor as well as Principal of a College for building up his/her institution is the recruitment of teachers.

Teaching in higher education is not mere dispensation of knowledge but development of independent creative thinking ability, social consciousness and commitment to the common weal and national integration along with a good value system. Better qualifications and UGC scales of pay have boosted the image of teacher in higher education. Committed teachers, with internal locus of control, contribute effectively to intrinsic and extrinsic student motivation. Unhealthy factors such as strikes and student indiscipline are minimized or eliminated completely when such disciplined teachers with their integrated styles of leadership are available, maximizing work in a humane atmosphere is possible with these excellent people. Such teachers follow the participatory methods of teaching and utilizing the best educational technology.

It is important that teachers shall be required to continuously update and upgrade their stock of knowledge through a well-organized mechanism of in-service training programmes at regular intervals. A well planned system of in-service training programme utilizing both conventional and distance mode and strengthening and networking of institutions at different levels may help to prepare such professionals.

ACADEMIC STAFF COLLEGE

Hawes and Hawes (1982) have given the following meanings of the term academic: (a) Institutional system of formal education within a school, college or university; (b) Theoretical, and not of practical importance and (c) A scholarly person who works in higher education. For the purpose of the present study, the third meaning that defines academic as a scholarly person who works in higher education has been adopted. Gene (1982) has given the following meanings of the term staff:

(a) The body of persons employed by an educational institution, or other organisation; some subgroup of those persons, as in guidance staff, or instructional staff,

(b) The act of recruiting and hiring those persons; and

(c) In a large organisation, the executives and specialists engaged in service and advisory function rather than in direct managerial and operative functions; in education, those in such staff functions include curriculum specialists, guidance counselors, and health care personnel. For the purpose of the present study, the term "staff' has been taken to mean a body of persons employed by an educational institution.

Therefore, the term "academic staff' taken together refers to the scholarly persons employed in an institution of higher education. In this sense, the term academic staff becomes synonymous with the term "faculty". The term faculty is derived from the Latin word Faculties which means ability, natural aptitude, and power or authority. When education got institutionalized and teaching was professionalised, the teachers got grouped and categorised as faculty in general, and in groups of related subject in particular (Knowles, 1977). However, one distinction can be drawn between the two terms "academic staff" and "faculty" which otherwise have been used interchangeably both in the literature and in the present study. Whereas the term "faculty" is used both for the teaching staff of an institution as well as the institution itself, the term "academic staff" is used in the former sense.

According to Amir Awang (1981), the term academic staff encompasses the whole range of academics, ranging from the position of lecturer to that of professor and it serves to distinguish teaching staff from administrative staff, general staff and technical staff. Normally, academic staff are classified into seven main categories: a) Lecturer; b) Senior Lecturer or sometimes known as Associate Professor; c) Reader; d) Professor, which includes visiting professors; e) Fellows on inter university exchange programme; f) Fellows who choose to spend their sabbatical in the university to conduct lectures, seminars or workshops for students; and g) Part-time lecturers who assist the scholarly centres in professional duties, especially teaching.

Teacher education has always been recognized as one of the most crucial means for social and national development. In the Indian context, this view has been endorsed by several commissions and committees appointed after independence. Recently, endorsing this view, the National Policy on Education (NPE)-1986 emphasised that the professional improvement and career enhancement of university and college teachers should be addressed on a continuous basis. As a result of this, 45 Academic Staff Colleges (ASCs) were established in 1987 in India. The Commission probably felt that Indian education couldn't achieve its avowed purpose unless it motivates and orients its teachers for academic excellence through self-development and innovation. Academic Staff Colleges propose to enhance the motivation of university and college teachers through systematic and organized orientation programmes, seminars and symposia that will enable them to discover their roles in the total socio-intellectual and moral ambience in which they operate.

Academic Staff Colleges, still emerging as structures for teacher orientation at the university stage, are intended to be the major agents to bring about the desired change and development in higher education. Such development, according to the University Grants Commission's (UGC) VII Five Year Plan Proposals, involves improvement in the management system of higher education and affecting a closer linkage between higher education and society through meaningful research. As already suggested, ASCs are intended to monitor and mediate these changes.

Education is a skilled profession; like any other skilled profession, training for the job has been widely accepted as an essential qualification for new entrants. Hence, training school teachers have been in practice for long in India. This concept of training, which has been universally accepted, is now being increasingly applied to, or considered for institutions of higher learning through orientation courses and refresher courses in India as well as abroad. It is with this aspect of teaching in mind that face-to-face orientation programmes for university and college teachers are organized at the ASCs for newly appointed lecturers followed by refresher programmes for in-service teachers. In other words, an ASC is a professional training institute, which imparts formal training in packages either of orientation programmes or refresher courses to newly appointed and in-service university and college teachers, respectively.

Orientation programme, here, refers to a short course/ programme designed to introduce teachers at the tertiary level to a subject, course etc. with a view to enabling them to discover their roles and potentials. This scheme also aims at equipping a teacher not just with the professional know - how but also with a certain outlook inhering a deep social commitment. This programme is a well - intended departure from the conventional pedagogy - oriented teacher training courses. Moreover, it is designed to bring about qualitative improvement in the educational standards and to make higher education variously meaningful and relevant to the present day society.

With regard to the orientation programmes, the U.G.C. states that "it is believed that the newly appointed lecturers not only need to be oriented to become effective teachers, but that most of them are already highly motivated to acquire the basic skills necessary for becoming successful teachers". The orientation programme, therefore, must engender in the teacher awareness of the problems that the Indian society faces and the role of education in the resolution of these problems, as well as in the achievement of the goals set out in the Indian constitution. Further matters relating to subject knowledge and pedagogy, although important in themselves, would be meaningful only when understood in the total context of national development. Similarly, in support of the refresher courses, the NPE envisages that "in addition to orientation courses for newly appointed lecturers, refresher courses will be organized for all serving teachers in colleges and university departments. The refresher courses will provide opportunities for serving teachers to exchange experiences with their peers and to mutually learn from each other. Refresher courses will also provide a forum for serving teachers to keep abreast of the latest advances in the various subjects. With the introduction of orientation and refresher courses, it is hoped that the culture of learning and self-improvement will become an integral part of educational system at the tertiary level"

GENESIS OF THE ACADEMIC STAFF COLLEGE

The idea of establishing Staff Colleges for the professional orientation of the university and college teachers was mooted, for the first time, by the University Education. Commission (1949). The commission recognized that the success of any education system would largely depend on the character and ability of the teacher and hence the teacher at the tertiary level should be prepared for:

(a) Transmission of the intellectual and ethical heritage of humanity to the young.

(b) Enrichment of this heritage and extension of the boundaries of knowledge, and

(c) Development of personality.

Although the commission recognized the training of teachers at the tertiary level, it remained silent on the establishment of the Academic Staff Colleges.

During 1960-61, the University Grants Commission started financing a number of universities and colleges for organizing symposia, summer schools and refresher courses. It was extended during the Second Five Year Plan. According to the UGC report for 1960-61, a few summer schools and refresher courses were organized in Mathematics and History of Science.

The report of the Education Commission (1964-66), with regard to the orientation programmes for university and college teachers, states, "an important point of emphasis would be the reorientation of university teachers to adopt new and improved techniques of teaching and evaluation. A programme of seminars, discussions or workshops should be organized to serve as the spearhead of the reform. The commission, however, suggested the following principles on which the training of tertiary level teachers should be attempted:

1. orientation of subject knowledge;
2. vitalization of professional studies;
3. improvement in methods of teaching and evaluation;
4. development of special courses and programmes; and
5. revision and improvement in curricula.

The Commission in this regard further stated that:

1. Newly appointed lecturers should be given some time and opportunity to acclimatize themselves to the institutions to learn the traditions and pattern of work, to get to know their colleagues and students:

    (a) They should be expected to study the syllabus carefully, to prepare a detailed programme for the teaching work they have to undertake to draw up their schemes of lectures, consult the library and select books to be recommended to students.

    (b) They should discuss these with the heads of their departments and senior colleagues and invite their suggestions.

(c) They should be encouraged to attend the lectures of some senior teachers of their subjects and study their methods of teaching and ways of handling their students.

(d) After the lectures, the senior teacher can discuss his methods and techniques with his junior colleagues who should be free to express their opinion and raise questions.

2. Every university and college should have regular orientation courses organized for a few weeks early in the session in which some new and senior older teachers participate.

3. The best teacher of the institutions as well as some distinguished teachers from outside should discuss with them the outstanding problems of teaching, research and discipline as well as the mechanics of the profession.

4. In bigger universities it may be possible to establish something like a staff college where teachers from all affiliated and constituent colleges as well as the university will be brought together for orientation, discussion, seminar, workshop, etc; and

5. Where this is not possible, a conference centre would be necessary to facilitate discussion of the issues, which teachers have to face, (e.g., objective of education, methods of teaching, enrichment of subject matter etc.).

Unfortunately, in spite of the clear recommendation for the establishment of academic staff colleges by the Education Commission, the idea lay in hibernation for almost two decades. Nothing beyond some refresher courses, conferences and need-based workshops were organized here and there during the period 1966 to 1986. Of course, as already mentioned, four universities had launched formal diploma or other courses in higher education.

As a result of the emphasis laid on the need of teacher development in higher education by the Education Commissions for the improvement and maintenance of the quality of education, the issue of faculty development started getting considerable attention from all quarters by 1970s and a number of quality development programmes were started by a few institutions. The Maharashtra Government had initiated a scheme of training for lecturers of junior colleges; the campuses of Bombay and Poona Universities ran regular courses on teaching methods for college lecturers; the Calicut University initiated a pre-service course of Master of College Teaching (MCT); the Department of Education of the University of Madras, on the other hand, initiated an in-service course of university teaching methods for the lecturers; similar courses were being contemplated by the Osmania University and Mysore University; M.S. University of Baroda decided in 1975 to start an in-service training on methodology of teaching at university level for fresh and newly appointed lecturers.

Besides these individualized attempts by some universities, the University Grants Commission, too, initiated a number of programmes at national level for quality improvement and promotion of excellence in teaching and research. Some of such programmes are as under:

- The programme of summer institutes, seminars, refresher courses and academic conferences was initiated to update teachers' knowledge in their respective fields of work and to update them with modern curricula and techniques of instruction to enable them to improve their professional competence.

- It initiated a scheme in 1970-71 to organise orientation courses for juniors and fresh lecturers in methods of teaching

- College Science Improvement Programme (COSIP) was initiated in 1971 for bringing about qualitative improvement in the teaching of science subjects at the undergraduate level in the affiliated colleges by a multi-pronged approach which involved improvements in the subject-matter, methods of instruction, syllabi, curricula, laboratory exercises, workshops, library and teaching materials. As on 31st March 1994, COSIP was being implemented in 314 colleges.

- Another scheme, College Humanities and Social Science Improvement Programme (COHSSIP), was started in 1974-75. New teaching methods, extension of library services, interdisciplinary programmes, examination reforms, remedial teaching and field/project work etc. were introduced as part of this programme. Up to 31 March 1992, 685 colleges (including 50 teacher training colleges) had been assisted in the first phase and 99 in the second phase of the programme.

- University Leadership Programme was established by the UGC to promote interaction between the faculties of selected departments of university with similar departments of colleges affiliated to it so as to enhance the professional competence of college teachers. It also started some other Faculty Improvement Programmes in 1974 under which the teachers were to be trained for the Ph.D. degree since it was taken as axiomatic that Ph.D. teachers would be better than non-PhD. teachers.

Though it is not difficult to define the methods for academic development or improvement, it is difficult to articulate and implement the methods for the development of professional skills of teachers in higher education. This is why the concept of professional development, which is so vital for a university set up, has gained momentum in our system though the need for it has been emphasized time and again. Professional development remained a policy of temptation and could not achieve the desired result. Joshi and Singh carried out a survey in 1978 to find out a systematic picture of the orientation programmes for the college and university teachers. The survey showed that the training of some sort was provided in eighteen Indian universities for their own teaching staff; fifty-four universities reported that they provided no training; two universities reported that it was under consideration and thirty-nine did not complete the questionnaire.

The National Commission on Teachers (NCT) in Higher Education, 1983-85, pointed out that the strategies to improve the faculty had not met with the desired success as only about two-thirds to three-fourths of the college teachers and one-third to half of university teachers participated in any seminar, summer school/workshop, training programme or research project; and hardly a quarter of either college or university teachers availed of study leave.

Because of the limited success of the individualized attempts by some universities and of UGC's schemes to revitalize the faculty, the NCT called for the following steps:

- At the Master's degree course itself, a few courses which were specifically related to teachers training could be offered as optional to those students who would like to enter the teaching profession later on.

- Again, Doctoral students could have some actual experience in teaching as in case of teacher assistants in the USA and as is required by the UGC in the case of junior fellowship holders.

- Lifelong, recurrent or in-service education of teacher was a must for his/her professional development and sufficient opportunities should be made available for it. These opportunities could be made available at the institution level but these seemed to be very limited. As such, the setting up the centres for professional development would be of great help.

The Mehrotra Committee in its report, re-emphasised the need of professional development of teachers and suggested the organisation of:

(i) orientation programmes for new teachers, and

(ii) refresher courses for teachers in general which should focus on two main facets:

(a) exposure to newer materials, and

(b) better way of disseminating the existing and new knowledge.

The year 1986 was a year of vigorous activity in the field of education; and it will go as a landmark of reforms and innovations in the history of Indian education. This year for the first time a "National Policy on Education" was drawn at the initiative of the central government. The National Policy on Education -1986 recognizing the role and importance of higher education observed "higher education provides people with an opportunity to reflect on the critical social, economic, cultural, moral and spiritual issues facing humanity. It contributes to national development through dissemination of specialized knowledge and skills. It is, therefore, a crucial factor for survival. Being at the apex of the educational pyramid, it has also a key role in producing teachers for the education system"(NPE, P.24, Para 5-24).

Thus, the policy framers not only recognized the role of higher education in producing teachers for the educational system but were also conscious about the quality of the teachers and their teaching. In this regard it was stated in the policy document "a major effort will be directed towards the transformation of teaching methods. Audio/visual aids and electronic equipments will be introduced; development of science and technology curricula and materials, research and teacher orientation will receive attention. This will require preparation of teachers at the beginning of the service as well as continuing education thereafter" (P. 15, Para 5-31).

In this way, the policy planners not only laid emphasis on the professional orientation of teachers in the beginning of their career but also desired a continuing reorientation from time to time during their teaching career. The importance given to the professional preparation and reorientation of university teachers is reflected in the NPE Programme of Action, when it states:

> *"The present system does not accord teachers a proper economic and social status, opportunities for professional and career development, initiative for innovation and creative work, proper orientation in concept, techniques and value system to fulfill their role and responsibilities. Motivation of teachers is important for the implementation of the policy" (p. 24, Para 15).*

To achieve this aim of professional orientation of the newly appointed teachers in the universities and colleges, and for the continuing reorientation throughout their teaching career, the NPE proposed the following measures in its Programme of Action for implementation.

(i) To organize specially designed orientation programmes in teaching methodology, pedagogy, educational psychology, etc. for all new entrants at the level of lecturers;

(ii) To organize refresher courses for serving teachers to cover every teacher at least once in 5 years;

(iii) To organize programmes by using the internal resources of universities and by bringing a number of colleges together;

(iv) To encourage teachers to participate in seminars, symposia, etc. and

(v) To promote self-learning among teachers through special programmes of the Open University.

Naturally, the UGC, being the apex body in the field of higher education, was entrusted with the job of launching a scheme of professional orientation and refresher courses for the university and college teachers in line with the expectations of the NPE. Further, the Government of India in its Seventh Five Year Plan draft proposals document "Development of Higher Education" made a pointed reference to this effect. The UGC in consonance with the Seventh Five Year Plan proposals and with a view to implementing the NPE Programme of Action formulated, in the first instance, a scheme for the orientation of newly appointed university and college teachers. The UGC while launching this scheme declared that "Under this scheme called the Academic Staff Orientation Scheme (ASOS), the UGC will support the VII Five Year Plan, the establishment of a number of Academic Staff Colleges, (ASCs) in different universities all over the county to plan, organize, implement, monitor and evaluate, on a regular basis, academic staff orientation programmes for newly appointed university and college lecturers. In the first stage, the UGC will support one ASC in every state. In larger states with greater number of newly appointed lecturers, the UGC may consider supporting more than one ASCs" (ASOS, UGC, P.4).

As a consequence, about 45 Academic Staff Colleges, totally funded by the UGC were established throughout the country in 1987 to offer professional orientation and refresher courses to the university and college teachers. Today, however, the total number of ASCs in the country has gone upto 57.

FUNCTIONS OF THE ACADEMIC STAFF COLLEGE

The functions of the ASC are highlighted below:

Induction Course

The change from student to beginning teacher is sudden and dramatic. From the supportive environment of the college, where mistakes are expected, self-criticism is encouraged, and both tutorial guidance and peer-group friendship are readily available, beginning teachers are thrust, only a few weeks later, into a situation in which both their professional and personal responsibilities are profoundly altered. There is a widespread agreement in certain countries that the first year should be the foundation of continuing professional education for teachers.

According to Zeichner (1979) the two major types of induction programmes are internship and beginning teacher programmes. Mc Donald (1982) defined internship as including: at least half-time teaching of no less than five or six months with full responsibility assigned to the interns for the group of classes which they teach.

Zeichner (1979) defined Beginning Teacher Programme as follows:

A planned programme, which is intended to provide some systematic and sustained assistance specifically to beginning teachers for at least one year. The persons providing support are specifically assigned that responsibility. In spite of the fact that though they are sometimes used synonymously still "Orientation" and "Induction" is not the same; on the whole, it probably makes most sense to regard orientation as an early stage in the overall induction process.

Orientation Course

The need of the day is to create a new generation of socially enlightened devoted teachers who should not only be highly knowledgeable persons in their respective disciplines, but also have their subject-oriented knowledge blended with social awareness and human qualities. For this purpose, the OPs were introduced for the newly appointed college and university teachers (originally below five years of service which was later extended to 8 years). These are the four week courses, and of the four major components, of the course curricula, three are broad-based and the fourth one, called the subject up gradation component, deals with specific subject of the individual teacher participant. The main objectives of these programmmes are (i) to make the relatively junior college and university teachers aware of the linkages between society, environment, development and education and the various socio-economic problems that our country is confronted with; (ii) to help them to realize the larger context of education and their role in our society; (iii) to make them aware of the significance of education in general and higher education in particular in the global and Indian contexts, philosophy of education, Indian educational system and pedagogy ; (iv) to familiarize them with the management of education ; (v) to promote in them personality development and to improve their skill of communication in the class-room lectures, and more importantly (vi) to inculcate in them a sense of accountability to the society, moral and ethical values of the teaching profession, strong integrity of character and human qualities, and (vii) to make them abreast of the latest developments in their respective disciplines. During the tenure of this four-week course, these teacher participants are involved in an extensive course of studies pertaining to different aspects of the aforesaid and related topics highlighted by a fairly large number of eminent resource persons.

Refresher Course

The Refresher Courses (RCs) are primarily subject-oriented and are introduced for the in-service teachers who have completed five years of service. The length of service of a teacher required for participation in a Refresher Course has now been reduced, provided he or she has already attended an Orientation Programme. A teacher can now participate in a Refresher Course one year after attending an Orientation Programme even before completion of five years of service in a substantive post. The main objective of these courses of 3-4 weeks duration is to keep the teacher aware of the new knowledge in their respective discipline that are continually proliferating at a tremendous rate and also to provide them an opportunity to refresh in their already acquired knowledge. If the teachers are not adequately updated with the new knowledge and information in their respective disciplines, the education of our student is bound to be out-dated and would eventually lose its relevance. During the tenure of these courses eminent resource (persons who are leading exponents in specific areas of a particular subject are invited to highlight the major latest developments in their respective areas of specializations. Listening to these highly informative and thought-provoking lectures delivered by the resource persons and interacting with them the participating teachers can get them refreshed in the existing knowledge and updated with the latest developments in their respective subjects to a great extent. In addition, each refresher course also includes participant-seminar sessions, in which each participating teacher is required to deliver a lecture on a topic directly related to his or her teaching curriculum, which is being evaluated by an eminent resource person. The knowledge acquired by the teachers from these courses is bound to raise the standard and quality of their teaching and is thus disseminated to the students who are considered to be the ultimate beneficiaries of these academic programmes. The importance of the RCs lies on how effectively this transmission of knowledge from the highest level to the learners in the college and universities is taking place. The quality of these courses is also an important factor. The ASC always takes particular care for the maintenance of the quality of its courses (both OPs and RCs) and works out a detailed programme for the evaluation of these courses by introducing various feedback processes. Both OPs and RCs conducted by ASCs are quite strenuous courses of studies.

SHORT-TERM PROGRAMME

The ASC also organizes short-term seminars/ workshops which are attended by leading educationists and other persons who are directly associated with higher education in various ways. The main objective of holding such seminars/workshops is to strengthen the ASC by involving them directly or indirectly with its academic activities. In addition, ASC also organizes special invited lectures on specific topics of current interest delivered by eminent scholars.

NEED FOR THE ORIENTATION PROGRAMME

The orientation programmes organized by the ASCs are meant for the newly recruited teachers at the university stage, who may one day after long years of experience, become effective teachers even without receiving this type of training. But an effort to organize and systematize the profession of teaching at this stage has to be scientific. The system cannot allow the newly appointed teachers to learn teaching on the job by trial and error. Effective teaching is based on sound methodology. So it is essential that the newly appointed teachers at the tertiary level be provided with the required scientific orientation. Such a course would enable them to overcome initial teaching difficulties apart from creating a sense of confidence among them; so that they can develop their own effective style of teaching. Teaching, to say the best, is a skilled profession and like any other skilled profession, training for the job should be an essential qualification for all new teachers.

Joshi and Singh (1978) found out that teacher orientation courses helped the development of teaching effectiveness in almost all the responded universities. In their study they also found that most of them have limited this orientation to new entrants, but a backlog of moderately experienced staff also should be taken care of. Thus, two types of courses, namely, (i) for new entrants and (ii) for experienced ones, were suggested.

Chalam (1987) suggested that the Academic Staff Orientation Scheme should have concentrated more on social relevant and productively useful syllabi and curriculum to save the system from decay. He further suggested that the Staff Orientation Programmes should be administered in three phases so that the participant could try the skills in his own institution and report to the training institution his experience.

Joshi (1987) pointed out the need for acceptance of the norm of successful participation in Academic Staff Orientation Course as the criterion for confirmation of the newly appointed lecturers.

Singh (1987) pointed out the importance of having desirable teacher trainers for successful administration of Academic Staff Orientation Programmes.

Passi and Sahoo (1988) conducted a study on a programme conducted by the Academic Staff College of Devi Ahilya University, Indore. The programme had 60 participants covering 22 subjects. There were 32 resource persons. The participants favoured short presentation followed by discussion, small group discussions and use of modern gadgets. They reported that the cyclostyled materials and handouts were not utilised by most of the participants. The researchers suggestion was for limiting the maximum number of participants in a programme to 30. They remarked that cultural programmes and two get together helped in sustaining the interest of the participants in the programme.

Das (1990) conducted a study on "Effectiveness of Self-learning Material for the Orientation of University and College Teachers" and found that when taught through the traditional teaching method, there was a significant gain in teachers' attitude towards orientation programme, professional awareness and academic achievement. Specifically, it was found that through traditional teaching method, the teachers' attitude became significantly more favourable towards the orientation programme, teachers' perceptions became significantly more favourable towards professional demands placed on them by their profession and their knowledge, understanding and application of the course content increased significantly.

Dhar and Singh (1990) in the book entitled "Academic Staff Colleges - A Developing Concept" have said that the philosophy, purposes and directions of Academic Staff Colleges must be understood by university teachers working from both sides of the table - standing as resource persons or sitting as participants. It has been envisaged that through professional and career development teachers can fulfill their role and responsibility within the educational system.

Both Dhar and Singh conducted a study on Academic Staff College established under Banaras Hindu University, which showed that even though most of the participants without knowing the utility of the programme, participated in with lukewarm zeal, it helped the bright ones in receiving reinforcement for furthering their insights. Intellectuals visualize new horizons in their own and allied disciplines. Dormant spirits were enkindled and sparked.

Pandey (1990) discussed about success of Academic Staff College of the Banaras Hindu University. It brought the four institutions of Varanasi closure and enlarged the knowledge and skills of the teachers.

Srinivasan (1990) pointed out the necessity of follow up programme for participants of orientation and refresher courses of the Academic Staff Colleges. The responsibility for follow up could be given to the Colleges of Education.

Despände and Jantli (1991) found that participants of Academic Staff Colleges displayed a significantly more positive attitude towards teaching.

Passi and Pal (1991) conducted a study on the relevance of the Academic Staff Colleges curricula. The topics not found useful by majority of the participants were youth and indiscipline, multi-lingualism, value based education, library study methods of evaluation, how to run a club and university management. Topics found useful were egalitarian society, philosophy of higher education, methods of teaching etc. They suggested inclusion of topics such as classroom control and psychological tests etc.

Passi and Rajendra Pal (1992) said that availability of qualified resource persons is regarded as essential for effective functioning of an Academic Staff College. Both Passi and Pal made an attempt to examine the perception of participants on the resource persons commissioned for Academic Staff Colleges.

The Institute of Education (IOE) Indore had organized orientation programmes for college and university teachers under the scheme of Academic Staff Orientation. Among the programmes 62 college teachers attended one. The duration of this course was of four weeks. The courses covered three curriculum components viz component A, component B and component D of Academic Staff Orientation Scheme. Component C i.e. subject up gradation was not included in the programme. The data were analysed by applying chi-square test to study the opinion of the participants. The researchers observed that those resource persons who used simple language for their presentation, created informal environment, encouraged discussions, distributed handouts, respected the participants in their class, were punctual in time, linked the topic in their day-to-day teaching etc. proved to be more effective.

Rehman and Biswal (1992) made an analysis over the participants' evaluation on the programmes of Academic Staff Colleges. The analysis was made on the basis of comparable information for only 12 Academic Staff Colleges covering 1372 participants of orientation programmes out of the total number of oriented participants during the year 1990-91. 85% of the total 336 respondents assessed the level of the programme conducted by the Academic Staff College as adequate, 12% as less adequate and rest 3% as not at all adequate. 43% of the total 1350 participants rated resource persons as very competent, 52% as competent and 5% as not so competent. Out of 1309 respondents 28% rated duration as "too long", 67% as "just alright" whereas 5% as "too short". Positive responses in various aspects of the programme by a large portion of participants were an indicative of the success of the programme.

Kapur (1992) found that the undergraduate teachers were interested more in listening to senior professors in their subjects rather than advanced or research topics, of which they see no immediate relevance for themselves.

Joseph (1993) analysed the functioning of Academic Staff Colleges vis-a-vis the course conducted by them and found that while in orientation course 50% of the time is to be spent on awareness of linkages between society, environment, education, Indian education system and pedagogy, management and personality development, 50% of the time is meant for subject up gradation. He made proposal for the introduction of "Teacher Development Courses" which will focus attention on teaching as a subject in the classroom, which entails both knowledge of the subject, techniques for transfer of knowledge and interaction strategies. It is said that during the course itself, the teacher can be familiarized in adapting the new techniques and to the extent possible; some of the difficulties faced by them could be solved through advice from the experts and discussions among peers. This can be an informal beginning of the follow-up work, very much needed for the success of any training programme.

Sethumadhava Rao (1993) presented the scenario of higher education system in India and paid stress on the transformation of the value system. He said that microteaching and group dynamic sessions should be introduced for the orientation courses. Besides, an objective yardstick is used while finalizing the micro details of the refresher courses. The Course Director regarding the grades secured by the participants of the college should inform the Principals of the colleges.

Rao and Palsane (1994) found that orientation programmes designed to improve the skills; the methods and broadening of attitude and horizon of the young teacher were useful and quantitatively successful. They also found out some classified content for such programmes. It was also pointed by Rao and others (1990) that there was a lot of variance in weightage given to different components of orientation programmes organized by the ASCs.

Passi and Pal (1994) tried to study the acceptability of the curriculum and curricular preference and found that to a great extent the curriculum was acceptable and the participant-teachers liked most of the topics. Rao, et., al examined the issue of adherence to UGC guidelines regarding curriculum and found that 64.25 percent ASCs followed the UGC guidelines beyond 75 percent. The remaining 35.75 percent ASCs had included other relevant topics keeping in view clientele nature and local reference. Some of the suggestions given while concluding their survey research by Rai and Rai (1995) were:

(i) There should not be any distortions of the UGC guidelines regarding the contents.

(ii) The Foundation course should consist of the role of higher education in the socio-culture dimensions. It should also be able to give a clear idea of the latest knowledge, techniques, principles and programmes of the educational world.

(iii) In the core course the teachers should be given knowledge about the latest principles and in-depth and thought on their concerned subjects.

(iv) Before starting the course, the outline of the course should be presented to the participants and their reactions and suggestions should be given a serious consideration.

(v) A continuous review and revision of ASC course should be taken up at various levels. Moreover, this should be followed by continuous surveys and research on such matters.

Kasinath and Pattel (1995) said that college teachers to be effective in their classrooms need professional training. They prepared a model for the purpose that is based on the analysis of professional preparation courses instituted in the Indian and Western Universities. Suggested model is named as Diploma in College Training (DCT). Duration of the course was decided as one year consisting of two semesters devoting the first semester to the study of theoretical aspects and the second to practical aspects with 20 weeks duration each. The model attempted to incorporate the modern trends like semester system, interdisciplinary approach, and continuous internal assessment, giving equal weightage to external and internal assessment and to different aspects of a course, lengthening the duration of the course.

Patil (1995) tried to evaluate the performances of Academic Staff Colleges on

(i) Attainment (for the objectives) of the Scheme of Academic Staff Colleges formulated by the UGC.

(ii) Achievements of the Academic Staff Colleges.

(iii) Constraints over the conduct of Academic Programmes.

On attainment of the Academic Staff Orientation Scheme (ABSOS), Patil suggested that the UGC should deal with various State Governments so that financial liability of the positions of Academic Staff Colleges can be taken over by the State Governments as soon as the UGC Scheme is over.

On achievement of Academic Staff Colleges he found that till March 1994 more than 967 Orientation courses and 1595 Refresher courses with 27675 and 43710 participants, respectively were held. Participants evaluated the courses as effective, relevant and useful to the academic development of teacher participants. He further said that the schemes of the Academic Staff Colleges have been appreciated and very well received by university and college teachers. Unfortunately, the Scheme has been unnecessarily tagged with the revised pay scales and therefore, in majority of the cases, the State Governments have made the participation of the university/ college teachers in the Refresher courses/Orientation programmes mandatory. In spite of this, a large number of college and university teachers responded very well to this Scheme and voluntarily participated in the courses organized by various Academic Staff Colleges.

Patil found that the inadequacy of physical facility has hampered a lot on the functioning of the Academic Staff Colleges and as a result the colleges are not in a position to offer the required number of refresher courses and orientation programmes expected by the UGC.

In many of the Academic Staff Colleges, the University professors have been asked to hold additional charge of the Director of the Colleges with an honorarium per month. Being preoccupied with their normal work they cannot spare the required time for the Academic Staff Colleges and it is likely that this could be one of the reasons for the deterioration of the quality of academic programmes of the Academic Staff Colleges.

Singh (1997) observed that the system of self-evaluation and routine monitoring has made the teachers realize that the fruit of this evaluation is professional development and self-empowerment. He said that adhoc nature of the institution of Academic Staff

College should be done away with. It must be accorded a permanent place in the university higher education system. Coordinators and resource persons should be given orientation about the interactive techniques of teaching. The Principals of colleges have to be convinced about the usefulness of such programmes.

Rastogi (1998) has said that universities play a central role in the development of the nation, as such special attention is to be given on preparation, training and up gradation of the university staff- both academic and administrative.

Academic Staff Development is considered as a process or intervention to bring about qualitative changes in the faculty to facilitate and improve the professional competence of individual faculty members in fulfilling their various obligations to achieve the goals and objectives of their institutions.

Vijayakumar (1998) has found that only a limited number of participants show keen interest in the orientation and refresher courses. Most of them attend the courses because of compulsion for obvious reasons. When teachers go for the refresher courses having 22 days duration, the regular work in colleges is affected. Vijayakumar suggested that participants should be selected based on interest in the area as evidenced by research work or teaching. The whole programme should be fully residential and the duration of the programme may be limited to seven days. Participants should be rated based on classroom participation, involvement etc.

Dutta (2000) expresses satisfaction over the functions of the Academic Staff Colleges as most of the colleges are able to achieve the objectives of Academic Staff Orientation Scheme.

A review on 15 aspects of orientation programms conducted by Sharma (2000) from 1988 to 1992 on 1842 teachers reveal positive responses from the teacher participants indicating the success of the programme. He has highly appreciated the Staff Development Programme initiated under the scheme of ASCs as a very important input for the development of excellence and relevance in the system.

Bhagabati (2002) conducted a study on "In-service Teacher Education At Higher Level With Special Reference To Guwahati

University Academic Staff College: An Evaluative Study" and found that the study results in positive feedback from majority of the participants. Specifically, it was found that the professional programmes conducted by Academic Staff College of Guwahati University have positive effect on advancement of knowledge and skills of teachers and provides a platform for sharing ideas. It was also found that the Academic Staff College, Guwahati University has achieved the objectives set forth by the Academic Staff Orientation Scheme.

Thus, it is clear from the above mentioned studies that the orientation programmes offered by the Academic Staff Colleges in India have resulted in significant gains in terms of acquiring knowledge, new skills and visions leading to effective presentation of the subject on the part of the university and college teachers.

Teaching and research are two main dimensions of higher education. For the development of a scientific methodology of teaching in any discipline, integration of teaching and research is essential. But unfortunately the two main dimensions of higher education, viz. teaching and research, have remained unintegrated so far. It is this state of affair that necessitates professional orientation of university and college teachers whereby they would be able to link research with the task of developing an effective methodology of teaching. This however, explains the second purpose of having teacher orientation at the university stage.

Ability for critical thinking, expressing and evaluating one's own ideas as well as those of others, tolerance for the views of others, and cooperating with others in any group work are some of the purported goals that a teacher has to keep in mind while organizing different learning activities for the university students. And for realizing these educational objectives, the methodology that the teacher is expected to adopt will form the core of the teacher education programme at the university stage. However, the ability of a teacher to adopt such a methodology cannot be isolated from what may be attempted in programmes of teacher education at stages prior to this: primary through higher secondary. This would mean that teachers directly admitted to the university/college stage will be required to orient themselves to features of teaching behaviour and teachers' functions in the previous stages (Yadav and Roy, 1977).

ACADEMIC STAFF COLLEGE: THE SCHEME

In line with the expectation of the NPE, the Academic Staff Orientation Scheme (ASOC) envisaged that "Every Academic Staff College will implement the programme of academic staff orientation on a regular basis. In the first stage, the orientation programmes for newly appointed lecturers may be undertaken followed subsequently by refresher programmes for serving teachers" (ASOS, UGC, 1987, P. 4).

In order to implement this scheme the UGC. prepared a set of guidelines and invited proposals from various universities with regard to the following aspects:

(a) Location of an Academic Staff College

As regards the location of the ASCs the UGC has laid down four possible formats in which these colleges could be established. They are:

(i) As a separate entity to be newly set up and designated within the university; or

(ii) As part of the existing department of continuing education; or

(iii) As part of college development council; or

(iv) In the form of a State Institute of Educational Planning and Administration.

In spite of the four possible formats suggested by the UGC, most of the universities preferred to adopt the first format. Thus most of the staff colleges have been established as separate entities in the university and have been designated as Academic Staff Colleges.

(b) Objectives of Academic Staff College

As regards the objectives of the Academic Staff Colleges, the

UGC expects that the orientation courses offered in these colleges will enable the newly appointed lecturers to:

(i) Understand the significance of education in general and higher education in particular, in the Indian and global context;

(ii) Understand the linkage between education and economic and sociocultural development with particular reference to the Indian polity where secularism and egalitarianism are the basic tenets;

(iii) Understand the role of a college/university teacher in the national goal of achieving a secular and egalitarian society;

(iv) Acquire and improve basic skills of teaching at the college/university level;

(v) Be aware of the developments in his specific subjects;

(vi) Understand the organization and management of a college/university and to perceive the role of a teacher in the total system; and

(vii) Utilize opportunities for development of personality, initiative and creativity (ASOC, UGC, P. 6).

(c) Curriculum for Academic Staff College

In order to achieve these objectives a curriculum framework was developed at the "National Workshop on Academic Staff College" held at the University of Bombay on 14th August 1987. This workshop conceived the curriculum for the Academic Staff College to have the following four components:

(i) Component A

Awareness of linkages between Society, Environment, Development and Education.

(ii) Component B:

Philosophy of Education, Indian Education System and Pedagogy.

(iii) Component C:

Subject Up gradation

(iv) Component D:

Management and Personality Development.

Component A

Awareness of linkages between Society, Environment, Development and Education.

This component should aim at helping the teacher to realize the larger context of education and the role of a teacher in a society. So illustrative topics to be covered are:

(i) Secularism;

(ii) Egalitarian Society;

(iii) National Integration;

(iv) Multilingualism;

(v) Multiple Cultures;

(vi) Equality,

(vii) Status of Women;

(viii) Casteism;

(ix) Environmental Pollution;

(x) Poverty;

(xi) Unemployment;

(xii) Urbanization;

(xiii) Modernization;

(xiv) Rural Development;

(XV) Youth;

(xvi) Indiscipline;

(xvii) Role and Responsibility of a Teacher;

(xviii) Value based Education;

(xix) Indian Tradition;

(XX) Creation of an Indian Identity.

Component B

Philosophy of Education, Indian Education System and Pedagogy.

This component should aim at imparting basic skills that a teacher needs for effective classroom teaching. Some of the illustrative topics are:

(i) Educational Philosophy-Aims and Objectives of Education, Role of an Educational Institution, Family and State in Education, Western and Indian Model;

(ii) Learner and the Learning Process-Human Growth and Development, Motivation, Group Psychology, Learning, Memory and Intelligence;

(iii) Indian Education Pattern-Organization of Central Ministry, State Ministry, Department of Education and Local Bodies,

(iv) School Education Pattern, Systems and Problems,

(v) Non-formal Education-Need and Organisation;

(vi) Economics of Education- Principles and Practices;

(vii) Sociology of Education-Education and Society;

(viii) Higher Education-Objectives, Organisation and Problems;

(ix) Curriculum Designs-Principles, Criteria of Utility, Variety and Flexibility, Principles of Individual Learning, Readiness and Mastery;

(x) Teaching Methodology-The Process of Teaching, Methods of Teaching, Types of Lessons, Lesson Planning, Skills in Teaching, Microteaching;

(xi) Evaluation Methodology-Concept of Measurement and Evaluation;

(xii) Classroom Techniques-Presentation, Lecture, Discussion, Seminar, Use of Black Board;

(xiii) Teaching Aids-Type of Aids, Appropriateness, Selection, Affectivity;

(xiv) Material Production - Supplementing the Text Book, Assignments, Quizzes, Term - papers; Reference and Study skills - Using a Library, Reference Skills, Self-study, Note Making, Review.

Component C

Subject Up gradation

This component should have two major thrusts:

(i) to enable the teacher to translate the relevant syllabus into a detailed plan of classroom presentation, and to effectively present the basic concepts at the appropriate level, and

(ii) to make the teacher self - sufficient in keeping himself continuously abreast of the new knowledge in his discipline.

Component D

Management and Personality Development

Under this component, attempts should be made to familiarize the teacher with the organisation and management at the college/

university level. The teacher should understand the interlocking of the various subsystems within the college/university and appreciate the role and functions of the teacher within the system. This part of component must be organized along the lines of programmes developed by the NUEPA.

Under component D the teacher should be made aware of the ways in which he may develop his own personality. The topics would include:

(i) Logical Thinking and Discussion;

(ii) Speech Training and Debating;

(iii) Public Speaking;

(iv) Communication Skills;

(v) Effective Writings;

(vi) Extra Curricular Activities;

(vii) How to run a Club/Society;

(viii) Sports;

(ix) Group Behaviour;

(x) Team Works; and

(xi) Student Counseling.

Although the workshop enlisted the topics under each of these components, as cited above, yet many of the ASCs have made certain changes and incorporated topics according to their local needs and availability of resource persons.

(d) Modality of Academic Staff Orientation Course

As regards the modus operandi to run these courses, it has been envisaged in the UGC Scheme that "an ASC will organize up to five - eight week orientation courses in one year. Each course will be attended by 40-50 newly appointed lecturers on full time basis" (ASOS, UGC, 1987).

The scheme further envisaged that "An orientation course will necessarily be full time and residential ...participating lecturers will be deputed by the respective college/university departments for the entire duration of the course. Since the 8 weeks period will be divided into two or three modules spread over a 12 to 18 months period, it should be possible for a college/university department to release new lecturers for two or four weeks at a time, twice or thrice in 18 months" (ASOS, UGC, 1987, p.8).

In order to make an orientation course optimally effective, the scheme states that the ASC will maintain a systematic record for all the participants, their achievements, their professional growth and above all, the changes in their capability as teachers.

(e) Monitoring and Evaluation of Academic Staff Orientation Programme

For the success of the academic staff orientation programme, it is necessary that every course should have an in - built monitoring and evaluation system. The division of every 8 weeks course into two or three modules would provide a convenient format for monitoring. Between any two modules, the participants should be assigned specific tasks and they should be required to submit assignments on the various components of the course as implemented by them in their day-to-day teaching and study. These assignments should be evaluated by course instructors and discussed with the participants as subsequent modules. The actual course should be progressively modified in the light of the information collected through such assignments.

For meaningful evaluation of a course three different kinds of evaluation may be carried out. They are:

(a) Self - evaluation by participants in terms of their own perceived attitudinal change and skill enhancement,

(b) Programme evaluation by the participants to evaluate the effectiveness of the programme,

(c) Formal evaluation of participants in terms of their achievement.

(f) Course Completion

It has been decided that it should be necessary to link the performance of participants at the course with career development. Therefore, it is recommended that confirmation of the newly appointed lecturers should be linked with the successful completion of an academic staff orientation course. Those lecturers whose achievement at a course is unsatisfactory should be permitted to go through the course a second time before confirmation. Those newly appointed lecturers who are already confirmed should be required to undergo the course.

In the form of the staff, a director heads each ASC. For each course, there is a provision for course coordinators. The post of the director is permanent and course coordinators are expected to be rotated amongst few well-identified academicians suitable for that particular course/module. Further, each ASC has an Academic Advisory Committee to advise on the orientation course and the selection of resource persons for delivering the course content to the participating teachers. On top of all this, the UGC has appointed a standing committee to guide/monitor/review the working of the ASCs. Thus, each ASC declares a list of the orientation courses along with their dates and the clientele focus. The colleges and universities coming in the territorial jurisdiction of the particular ASC depute their lecturers to attend the orientation courses. These teachers are paid TA and DA by the ASC, which they attend. Further, the ASC also invites resource persons to deliver the content of that course to the teachers. These resource persons are also paid TA and DA along with honorarium of Rs. 200 per lecture. In this way the ASCs achieve the objectives set forth for them through running 4 to 8 weeks long orientation courses, which are often divided into several modules with the help of resource persons who are invited from all over India.

NEED FOR THE STUDY

A positive outcome of the report of the Mehrotra Committee (1986) and National Policy on Education - 1986 has been the concerted effort of the University Grants Commission (U.G.C.) to set up 57 Academic Staff Colleges (ASCs) all over India.

The National Policy on Education (1986) had made a pointed reference to the crucial link between teacher performance and the quality of education. The Mehrotra Committee went beyond that and linked the promotion of the teachers from one scale to another with participation in orientation and refresher programmes.

The fact of the matter is that the importance of initial training and then continued retraining of teachers was emphasized as long ago as the mid-sixties. Even when the Fourth Plan was being drawn, the Task Force on Higher Education appointed by the Planning Commission mooted this idea. Something was done in consequence of this initiative. Over the years teacher fellowships and similar programmes were launched, but nothing like a system got evolved.

However, the haste with which the orientation programmes through the Academic Staff Colleges have been implemented since 1987 raises many misgivings. Till 1986 there was not even a single Academic Staff College. During 1987 a number of ASCs were established. This pace of activity might have given birth to a number of problems that have not been ascertained through empirical research till date.

Funding of the ASCs is, being very liberally, coming from the U.G.C. and is not a problem. But how these programmes are organized? What kind of a format has eventually got evolved? What quality of instructors become available and are engaged? What is the extent and degree of their motivation and capability? What is the nature and mode of support extended to the ASCs by senior administrators? are some of the factors that would determine the success or otherwise the failure of this experiment.

However, a real problem may be raised in terms of the format, which these colleges have evolved for themselves. No doubt, the kind and quality of staffs are going to be critical factors. Where are the instructors coming from and with what kind of background and outlook? What kinds of problems are encountered in the classroom and outside and how those can be dealt with?

Further, it has been made clear that each ASC should have five members of the core staff. It means at least 285 (57 x 5 = 285) people with right motivation, seriousness, and commitment towards the programmes will be needed. But, in the absence of sound empirical evidence it is difficult to ascertain the suitability of the core staff in terms of the qualities mentioned above.

In the absence of a national database and research evidence pertaining to the questions rose above, a study becomes very essential. Further, the experience and the personal involvement of this investigator in the orientation programmes of the ASC, Banaras Hindu University, for his Ph. D. Work entitled "Effectiveness of Self-learning material for the Orientation of the University and College Teachers," have been the decisive factor that motivated him to undertake this research work as this investigator has already come across with the inherent problems of the ASC stated above. In the light of this background the present investigation formally titled as:

"A Critical Evaluation of the Teaching - Learning Systems, adopted for the Orientation of the University and College Teachers in the existing Academic Staff Colleges in India"

is proposed by this investigator to fulfill this gap by seeking answers to the following questions :

1 What is the nature and mode of delivery of the orientation programmes provided by different Academic Staff Colleges?

2. What are the perceptions of the participants about the:

   (i) Nature, suitability and mode of delivery of the orientation programmes.

   (ii) Resource persons; and

   (iii) Improvement of the course content of the orientation programmes.

3. How far the practices adopted in the ASCs innovative in nature?

4. What are the areas where duplication in efforts and wastage of resources be avoided?

5. What guidelines are really required for the future improvements of the orientation courses in various ASCs?

OBJECTIVES OF THE STUDY

The above stated broad questions can be spelt-out in the form of following specific objectives, which the study will be focused to achieve:

1. To ascertain the nature and mode of delivery of the orientation programmes of ASCs with respect to:

Nature

(i) the content of the course and course materials;

(ii) the duration and organisation of the courses;

(iii) the co-curricular, organizational and financial aspects of the programmes;

(iv) the resource persons and their background relevant to the content of the course.

Mode of Delivery

(i) methods of presentation;

(ii) media and aids used;

(iii) interaction to participants offered.

2. To critically evaluate the aspects studied under objective 1 through the perceptions of the participating teachers in terms of:

(i) suitability of the content of the course and course materials;

(ii) suitability of the duration and organisation of the courses;

(iii) suitability of the co-curricular, organizational and financial aspects of the programmes;

(iv) resource persons and their background relevant to the content of the courses;

(v) suitability of the methods adopted for the presentation of the courses;

(vi) suitability of the media and audio-visual aids used;

(vii) suitability of the process of interaction among the participants and resource persons.

3. To study and compare the courses offered and facilities extended in the various ASCs in order to suggest viable strategies for avoiding duplication and wastage of resources.

4. To develop guidelines for the future improvements of the orientation courses.

SIGNIFICANCE OF THE STUDY

The study has made an in-depth analysis of the various teaching-learning systems adopted for the orientation of the University and the College Teachers in the existing Academic Staff Colleges in India. The systems specifically studied are: (a) nature of the course content and course materials, (b) duration and organisation of the course, (c) co-curricular, organizational and financial aspects of the programme, (d) resource persons and their background relevant to the content of the course, (e) methods of the presentation, (f) media and aids used, and (g) interaction to participants offered. Further, as these systems have been studied and critically evaluated at the national level in the light of the teachers' perceptions (who are the real beneficiaries of the system); the study is expected to present a critical holistic picture of the process of management of orientation programmes offered by the Academic Staff Colleges in India in a national perspective. Not only the strength of the systems of teachers' orientation at the tertiary level in India have been pointed out but also its weaknesses have been highlighted.

In this light, the study is expected to provide the much-needed research based data for planning the qualitative development of teacher orientation programmes at the tertiary level all over the country and avoid duplication and wastage of resources. In the study, each sub-system of orientation of university and college teachers in India has been analysed and evaluated in terms of teachers' perception. The results of this analysis have been synthesized and presented in separate chapters. Hence, this analytic synthetic approach has enabled the researcher to draw implications for improvement of the sub-system under study and reflect upon strategies that could be adopted to make the system cost effective.

DELIMITATIONS

For reasons beyond the control of the investigator and the impositions due to the availability of limited time and funds, the study was delimited in the following respects:

(a) A 25 percent sample of those Academic Staff Colleges was taken who had given their consent to participate in the study and were willing to supply the data needed for the study. Thus, while interpreting the results of the study the limitations arising out of the selection of a limited number of 12 Academic Staff Colleges, should be kept in mind.

(b) As the size of the population of teacher participants is very large and scattered all over the country, it was possible to take 765 participants from 12 selected Academic Staff Colleges, on an average of 63.75 teacher participants from each of the college selected. A further limitation that arose due to paucity of funds and time was that only one reminder was sent to those teacher participants who did not respond to the questionnaires in the first instance. The non-respondents were not substituted by a further sample. Thus, this limited number of teachers has been taken to represent the perceptions of the entire population of teachers oriented in the

Academic Staff Colleges in India. Lastly, staff development programme has been limited to only OPs.

CHAPTER-II

METHOD AND PROCEDURE

The study was basically concerned with two things: (a) survey of the systems adopted for the orientation of the university and college teachers in the existing ASCs; and (b) the evaluation of the existing systems to judge their suitability and effectiveness.

Two variants of survey method, mail and field survey were adopted. Field visits to ASCs provided data to achieve the first objective of the study. Through mail survey, information pertaining to the second objective was obtained from those participants who had undergone the orientation programmes offered by the ASCs and scattered geographically all over India.

The nomographic approach was adopted to some extent in surveying the process adopted for; (a) the preparation and delivery of the course content and course materials, (b) duration and organisation of these materials, (c) resource persons and their background relevant to the content of the course, (d) providing feedbacks to suggest viable strategies for the future improvements of the orientation programmes, and (e) evaluation of the participant teachers' performance at the national level. In adopting the nomographic approach, it was assumed that there are some general characteristics or traits, which can be applied to all the Academic Staff Colleges (ASCs). As such attempt has been made to express questions and reply categories in so general manner that they are applicable to as many ASCs as possible. In the light of the UGC guidelines for the introduction of the ASCs, it can be assumed that the ASCs in India do not differ significantly with respect to: (i) structure and organisation, (ii) nature of courses offered and (iii) educational system/traditions, etc. This facilitated the adoption of the nomographic approach as the same elements may be found in different ASCs. Thus, most of the questions and response categories will be equally relevant, with least scope of misinterpretation to all the ASCs.

It may be argued that the nomographic approach may provide only a superficial description of the system, but the method seems to be justified as a means to acquire basic information for want of systematic data on a large number of institutions. The idiographic approach may be advocated, but it is used in studies aiming at precise description of single institution to get a better fit between description and reality. However, these advantages of the idiographic approach were incorporated in this study to a great extent by visiting the ASCs and personally administering the survey questionnaires.

The evaluation of the surveyed systems, adopted by the ASCs for executing instruction and supporting learning at the national level, has been done against the following two criteria:

(i) The perceptions, reactions and needs of the participant teachers i.e. feedback received from teachers regarding various aspects of the system;

(ii) Theoretical discussion and comparison of 'what is' with 'what ought to be' in the light of the suggestions given by the participants.

In doing this evaluation, holistic mode of evaluation has been adopted to present the picture of the entire system in a national perspective. Sufficient care has been taken to point out the weaknesses, the strengths, and the areas where linkages and co-ordination can be established to tone up the system at the national level and avoid duplication and wastage in it.

POPULATION

The survey population included all the ASCs in India. Accordingly, university/college teachers oriented in these colleges constituted the population for getting participants' perception data for the evaluation of the teaching learning systems adopted in their respective ASCs. Although, at the time of data collection, there are 45 ASCs, which offer orientation and refresher courses, but only 12 universities came in the purview of this study. The Open Universities,

Agricultural Universities, Regional Colleges of Education and other institutes offering orientation and refresher courses have been kept out of the scope of the study. Of the 45 ASCs that came in the purview of this study, 13 were located in the northern region, 12 were located in the southern region, 8 in the eastern region, 9 in the western region and 3 in the central region of India.

SAMPLE

Of the 45 ASCs that came in the purview of the definition of population, 12 i.e. 25% were selected randomly ensuring the selection of at least one ASC from the North, South, East, and the West and the Central regions of India. From these 12 selected ASCs, 765 participants were selected randomly to be included in the sample. In this way, 12 ASCs and 765 participants selected from them constituted the sample of the study.

As already mentioned, because of the standard U.G.C. guidelines for the establishment of the ASCs in the university, much differences are not expected in the structure and organisation, level of course offered and the systems adopted by different ASCs. Of course some variations are expected to occur because of the cultural background and regional differences in the location of the ASCs. But as most of the ASCs are clustered in the northern regions of India, a sufficiently large sample from this region along with 2 from southern, 3 from eastern and also 3 from western region is expected to represent the defined population. Hence, 26% sample of the 45 ASCs which gave consent to participate in the study was selected as shown below in Table - 2.1:

Table- 2.1: Region-wise No. of ASCs Selected in the Sample

Region	No. of ASCs	No. Selected
Northern	13	4
Southern	12	2
Eastern	8	3
Western	9	3
Central	3	Nil
	Total Selected	12

Thus, 4 ASCs from the northern, 2 from the southern, 3 each from the eastern and western regions of India were selected randomly by lottery method from those who gave consent to participate in the study. In this way not only the cultural background variations were taken care of but also the regional location representation was ensured. The Appendix-I presents the details of the 12 ASCs on which this study was conducted.

As regards the sample of teachers, on an average, 63.75 teacher participants were selected randomly from each of the 12 selected ASCs. Thus, a total number of 765 university and college teachers constituted the sample for collecting data to be used for evaluating the systems of teaching and learning adopted for the orientation of the university and college teachers in the existing ASCs. The decision to include a limited number of teachers from each institution was taken under the constraints of limited funds available, increased postal rates and above all non-availability of teacher participants in the host institutions. However, the sample of 765 teachers can be considered to be a fairly representative sample of the total population, as it has been drawn strictly on random basis using table of random numbers, after procuring the address list of the teachers in the selected ASCs.

TOOLS

Two written questionnaires, developed by Das,(1999) were used to collect data and information for achieving the objectives of the study. They are:

(a) System of Orientation Programme Questionnaire (SOPQ), and

(b) Participants' Feedback Questionnaire (PFQ).

SYSTEM OF ORIENTATION PROGRAMME QUESTIONNAIRE (SOPQ)

It is a very comprehensive and to a large extent standardized questionnaire; meant for eliciting information and data about the teaching-learning systems adopted for the orientation of university/ college teachers in the existing ASCs, from the Director, Course Coordinators and the staff of the sampled institutions.

The covering letter accompanying the questionnaire contains some information about the purposes and significance of the study and a request for co-operating in the successful supplication of the study. The title page of the questionnaire has been designed in the manner of 'Total Design Method' suggested by Dillman (1987). It contains the theme and sponsorship of the project along with the name of the principal investigator (see appendix -III).

The questionnaire is very extensive, therefore, demands great effort on the part of those responding and contains 89 questions. Assuming that the same elements may be found in various ASCs, nomographic approach was adopted to structure the response categories of the standardized questions. The questions refer to the following general areas pertaining to the systems of teaching and learning adopted by the ASCs :

(a) general characteristics of the institutions,

(b) selection criteria,

(c) format for Academic Staff College,

(d) course content and course materials,

(e) organisation and duration of the course,

(f) finance,

(g) administration,

(h) resource persons,

(i) methodology followed in Orientation Programme,

(j) adoption of teaching media and aids,

(k) evaluation,

(l) set of problems pertaining to staff, participants, resource persons, course content, methodology, reading materials, finance and infrastructure,

(m) future plans about the development of the ASC.

PARTICIPANT'S FEEDBACK QUESTIONNAIRE (PFQ)

In order to get participants' reactions and opinions about the quality and suitability of the teaching learning systems adopted by the ASCs, the Participant's Feedback Questionnaire was developed by Das (1999). This questionnaire was basically designed to obtain data that could be used as feedback from the participants to evaluate the effectiveness of the systems.

It is a very comprehensive questionnaire having 54 questions, thus requiring a great effort on the part of the responding participants. The questionnaire was standardized to a great extent; but depending upon the nature of information required, free response questions had also been included, particularly when suggestions were invited. In a few questions the respondent has to supply information; while in some others he is required to select alternatives. The title page has been designed according to the "Total Design Method" (Dillman, 1987). It contains the theme and sponsorship of the project along with a covering letter highlighting the significance of the study and requesting to return of the duly filled questionnaire (See Appendix-IV).

In the questionnaire, the first 12 questions seek general information regarding some personal and demographic characteristics of the ASCs. The remaining 42 questions refer to following areas:

(a) compulsory or voluntary nature of the OPs, academic benefits of the OPs,

(b) suitability of the course content and course materials,

(c) suitability of the duration and organisation of the OPs,

(d) suitability of the co-curricular and financial aspects of the programme,

(e) suitability of the resource persons,

(f) suitability of the methods adopted, media and aids used, and interaction to participants offered during the OPs.

The last question of the questionnaire seeks suggestions from the participants for further improvement of the OP.

DATA COLLECTION AND RESPONSE RATE

Two types of data were required to achieve the objectives of the study:

(a) Institutional data from the existing ASCs pertaining to the teaching-learning systems adopted for the orientation of the university/college teachers in the ASCs; and

(b) Feedback data from the participants to evaluate the suitability and effectiveness of the system.

The SOP was administered personally on the staff of the selected ASCs and the PFQ was mailed to 1437 participants included in the sample. In order to ensure return, a self-addressed postage paid envelope along the questionnaire was sent to each participant.

As usual for mailed questionnaires, the problem of low response rate was faced in getting the data from the participants. Of the several reasons, the main reasons that seem to be responsible for this are: (a) postal problems, (b) comprehensiveness of the questionnaire and the complexity of the questions asked, (c) family responsibilities, etc. Hence, many participants could not put the effort required to respond to a rather demanding questionnaire.

After a reminder to those participants who did not respond to the questionnaire in 30 days, a response rate of 53.23% was achieved. For a mailed questionnaire, an overall response rate of 53.23% can be considered quite satisfactory. However, it may be noted that the number of respondents varies from question to question, either due to non-response to the question or that the question was not applicable in same cases.

Table - 2.2: Response Rate of Participants

S.No.	Name of the ASCs	Questionnaire		Response Rate
		Posted	Returned	
1.	Delhi University	120	66	55.00%
2.	Utkal University	105	61	58.10%
3.	Mysore University	118	75	63.56%
4.	Madras University	114	71	62.28%
5.	University of Gujarat	137	83	60.58%
6.	Panjab University	127	60	47.24%
7.	University of Kashmir	118	48	40.68%
8.	Gauhati University	136	81	59.56%
9.	Himachal Pradesh University	132	76	57.58%
10	Calcutta University	115	48	41.74%
11.	Mumbai University	105	51	48.57%
12.	Pune University	110	45	40.91%
	Total	1437	765	53.23%

TABULATION OF DATA: SOME PROBLEMS AND POSSIBLE ERRORS

The questionnaires used in this study are standardized to a great extent, but they also contain some open-ended questions; tabulation of answers to these questions showed low inter-rate concordance. Hence, the frequencies for these answers are often not reported; but whenever they have been reported - a wide variety of responses have been condensed into manageable number on the basis of similarity in responses.

The coding and tabulation of the answers to other types of questions is also susceptible to errors, however. The reasons for this are:

(a) Not all questions and response categories, particularly in the students' feedback questionnaire, seem to be clear. This is evident from students' comments, which point to misunderstandings caused by some of the wording of a few questions.

(b) Not all questions and response categories are applicable to all the institutions; thus the number of respondent (N) varies for such questions while tabulating frequencies.

(c) In some cases of students' response, answers to related questions are contradictory i.e., some contradictions in responses have been observed.

(d) In some cases of students' response, comments or opinions expressed on categories ticked off conflict with the chosen category.

(e) Although the questionnaires in which response set or faking was noticed were disregarded yet there may be some responses, which fall in this category.

Some of these ambiguities were cleared up by considering the context and information revealed by in the response of fellow participants of the same institution, dangers of error might still remain.

Mostly frequencies and percentages have been used to tabulate and analyze the responses to the questions in the questionnaires.

CHAPTERISATION OF THE RESULTS

There are three main objectives of the study: the first is concerned with the survey of the systems, and the second and the third are concerned with the evaluation of these systems in the light of teachers' perceptions and latest developments in the area of orienting university and college teachers in the ASCs in India. The achievement of the first two objectives demands an empirical analysis of the data yielded by the questionnaires used in the study. The achievement of the third objective calls for a theoretical comparison of the courses offered by the ASCs in India. Instead of analyzing data and presenting the result of this analysis separately for each objective, the analysis of data has been synthesized. The purpose of this synthesis is to present the evaluated picture of the systems adopted for the management of various aspects/ components of orientation programmes in a holistic perspective at the national level. However, for the sake of clarity in presentation each subsystem corresponding to the objectives of the study has been analysed and evaluated separately under the following headings in independent chapters:

Chapter 3: Selection of Participants

Chapter 4: Course Content and Course Materials

Chapter 5: Organisation, Administration and Duration

Chapter 6: Co-curricular and Financial System

Chapter 7: Resource Persons.

Chapter 8: Methodology Followed

Chapter 9: Evaluation System

Chapter 10: Problems

Chapter 11: Future Plans

Chapter 12: Major Findings and Suggestions

CHAPTER-III

SELECTION OF PARTICIPANTS

This Chapter has been designed to address to some of the questions that often come to our mind ever since the establishment of the ASCs in India. For instance, what should be the intake capacity of the OPs? What criteria and procedure are followed for the selection of teachers? Is the catchment area demarcated by the UGC for inviting participants sufficient? Do some participants seek admission to the course repeatedly? What should be the approximate period between successive courses for selection and what format has really been evolved for the establishment of the ASCs in India?

INTAKE CAPACITY

As regards the intake capacity of one orientation programme, the Director and the staff of the ASCs were asked a question: "what should be the reasonable intake capacity of one orientation programme?" They were provided with four possible alternatives to respond.

The results in Table 3.1 show that in case of 29.17% ASCs, intake capacity for one orientation programme should be 30 to 35; it should be 35 to 40 for 20.83% ASCs; 41.67% ASCs state that intake capacity for one OP should be 40 to 45; and it should be 45 to 50 in case of only 8.33% ASCs.

Table - 3.1: Intake Capacity of One Orientation Programme

SOPQ: What should be the reasonable intake capacity of one Orientation Programme?		f	%
(a)	30-35	07	29.17
(b)	35-40	05	20.83
(c)	40-45	10	41.67
(d)	45-50	02	8.33
		N=24	

SELECTION CRITERIA

Selection of teachers for participation in the OPs is a crucial issue. The criterion followed in the selection of participants was found out in the present study. For this purpose, the staffs of the ASCs were asked whether they followed any strict criteria for the selection of teachers or not. The results given in Table 3.2 indicate that almost all (95.83%) of the ASCs in India follow strict criteria for the selection of teachers, while in the case of 4.17% ASCs, no criteria is followed for the selection of teachers for the OPs in India.

Further, the staffs of the ASCs were also asked to reveal the selection criteria followed in their institutions. They were provided with a list of five possible criteria for the selection of teachers in the OPs and were asked to give tick mark to the criteria, which applied in the ASCs. An open-ended response was also provided to seek any other criteria if applied besides those mentioned in the questionnaire. The results in the same Table 3.2 indicate that two of the every three ASCs (66.67%) observe that lists of the fresh teachers in universities/colleges from the catchment areas are invited. Again, only in 20.83% cases, subjects are selected and teachers of that particular subject are invited to the OPs; in 37.50% cases, only those teachers are invited who are appointed on substantive posts; while only 4.17% of the ASCs invite educational administrators (Head, Dean and Principal) for the selection of the teachers in the OPs. It is interesting to note that in 62.50% cases,

ASCs also invite participants from outside catchment areas for the participation in the OPs.

Moreover, the staff of the ASCs also mentioned some other criteria adopted by them in the selection of teachers for the OPs such as; (i) the requirements of the participants; (ii) 10% teachers from outside catchment areas and (iii) seniority in the subject.

Table - 3.2: Criteria for the Selection of Teachers

SOPQ: Do you follow any strict criteria for the selection of teachers?		f	%
	Yes	23	95.83
	No	01	4.17
SOPQ: Which of the following criteria for the selection of teachers is applied to your ASC?			
(a) A list of the fresh teachers in universities/colleges from the catchment areas are invited.		16	66.67
(b) Subjects are selected and teachers of that particular subject are invited.		05	20.83
(c) Only those teachers are invited who are appointed on substantive posts		09	37.50
(d) Educational Administrators (Head, Dean and Principal) are invited.		01	04.17
(e) Participants from outside catchment areas are invited.		15	62.50

N = 24, but multiple responses possible.

PROCEDURE FOLLOWED

As regards the procedure followed for the selection of teachers for OPs of ASCs, the results presented in Table 3.3 reveal that no ASC conduct interview of those who apply for participation in the OPs; only 4.17% out of 24 respondents opine that Advisory Committee is there to screen the candidates on the basis of their bio-data; and similar number of respondents, i.e., 4.17% indicate that the Director and Deputy Director in consultation with the Course Coordinators select the participants for the OPs. However, most of the ASCs in India (91.66%) follow strictly the UGC norms for selection of teachers for OPs.

Table-3.3: Procedure Followed in the Selection of Teachers

SOPQ. Procedure followed for Selection,	f	%
(a) Interview is conducted of those who apply,	00	N.A.
(b) Advisory Committee screens the candidates on the basis of their bio-data	01	4.17
(c) UGC norms are strictly followed	22	91.66
(d) Director and Deputy Director in consultation with the Course Coordinators select the participants	01	4.17

N = 24

SUFFICIENCY OF CATCHMENT AREAS

The staffs of the ASCs were asked to respond a question: "Is the catchment area of your college demarcated by the UGC for inviting participants sufficient?" The results given in Table 3.4 show that in case of most of the ASCs, i.e. 83.33%, the catchment area demarcated by the UGC for inviting participants is sufficient. It was only in case of 16.67% ASCs, the catchment area is not sufficient as demarcated by the UGC for inviting participants for the OPs. So, it may be concluded that majority of the ASCs (62.5% in Table 3.2) invite participants from outside catchment area due to the fact that participants within the catchment area are not sufficient.

Table-3.4: Sufficiency of the Catchment Area for Participants

SOPQ: Is the catchment area of your college demarcated by the UGC for inviting participants sufficient?		f	%
	Yes	20	83.33
	No	04	16.67

N = 24

REPEATED ADMISSION

With an intention to find out whether or not participants seek admission to the course repeatedly, the staffs of the ASCs were asked a question: "Do some participants seek admission to the course repeatedly?" The results indicate (Table -3.5) that most of the respondents i.e. 79.17% report that some participants seek admission to the OP repeatedly; whereas, every fifth respondents (20.83%) do not want the same.

Again, one more question in the questionnaire pertaining to prevention of repeated admission of the participants to the OP was asked to the staff of the ASCs. The results in Table - 3.5 show that majority of the respondents (58.33%) state that participants are prevented for taking admission to the courses for second time; while every fifth respondents (20.83%) report that their colleges do not prevent the teachers seeking admission for the second time.

Table - 3.5: Seeking Admission to the OPs for Second Time

SOPQ: Do participants seek admission to the course repeatedly?	f	%
Yes	19	79.17
No	05	20.83
SOPQ: If yes, do you prevent them for admission to courses for second time?		
Yes	14	58.33
No	05	20.83

N = 24

PERIOD BETWEEN SUCCESSIVE COURSES

The responses of the staff of ASCs to one question regarding stipulation of period between successive courses reveal that about four of every fifth respondents (79.17% in Table - 3.6) report that a minimum period is stipulated between successive courses for selection; while every fifth respondents (20.83%) observe that no such stipulated period between successive courses is followed by them.

Moreover, the respondents who revealed that a minimum period was stipulated between successive courses (79.17%) were asked one more question relating to approximate period between successive courses. The result presented in the Table - 3.6 indicate that only 8.33% respondents report that the approximate period between successive courses for selection is 10 months; it is 1 year as stated by most of the respondents (58.33%); and in case of 12.50% respondents, it is 2 years.

Table - 3.6: Approximate Period between Successive Courses for Selection.

SOPQ: Have you stipulated a minimum period between successive courses for selection?		f	%
	Yes	19	79.19
	No	05	20.83
SOPQ: If yes, please give the approximate period between successive courses for selection.			
	10 months	02	8.33
	1 year	14	58.33
	2 years	03	12.50

PARTICIPATION OF SELECTED TEACHERS

As regards participation of selected teachers, the responses of the staff of the ASCs reveal that three of every fourth respondents, i.e. 75% in Table - 3.7 observe that the participants selected by ASCs for a given course attend the same as expected. However, every fourth (25%) state that the selected participants do not attend the OP as expected. So the question that arises at this stage is what are the reasons for which selected participants do not attend the OP as expected? The responses of the staff involved in the ASCs to this question reveal that the selected participants do not attend the OP as expected, because (a) circulars sent about the conduct of orientation courses to the Principals/Heads are not shown to the teachers (16.67%), (b) Principals/Heads are reluctant to relieve teachers in time (25%), (c) Teaching in the parent departments suffers during the period teachers are relieved to participate (8.33%), (d) Teachers selected to attend the course do not join at the last moment (20.83%), and (e) some of the teachers lack sufficient motivation to attend the OPs (8 33%). From this observation, it is evident that Principals, Heads and teachers themselves - all are responsible for non-participation of selected teachers in the OPs organized by the ASCs in India.

Table - 3.7: Participation of Selected Teachers

SOPQ: Do you think that participants selected by your college for a given course attend the same as expected?		f	%
	Yes	18	75.00
	No	06	25.00
SOPQ: If not, please mark (√) the following reasons best known to you:			
(a)	Circulars sent about the conduct of Orientation Courses to the Principals/Heads are not shown to the teachers	04	16.67
(b)	Principals/Heads are reluctant to relieve teachers in time	06	25.00
(c)	Teaching in the parent departments suffers during the period teachers are relieved to participate	02	08.33
(d)	Teachers selected to attend the course do not join at the end/ last moment	05	20.83
(e)	Some of the teachers lack sufficient motivation.	02	08.33

N = 24

FORMAT FOR ACADEMIC STAFF COLLEGE

The responses of the staff involved in the ASCs to a question regarding the format evolved for the establishment of ASCs indicate that all the respondents (100% as given in Table - 3.8) report that ASC has been established as a separate entity within the university. Of course, there are some other alternative formats for ASCs such as, (a) ASC has been established as a part of an existing department of continuing education; (b) ASC has been established as a wing of the College Development Council; and (c) ASC has been established in the form of a State Institute of Educational Planning and Administration. But no respondents report in favour of these alternative formats. It is clear that, ASCs have been established as separate entity within the university and have been provided with academic autonomy and availability of internal resource persons, etc.

Table - 3.8: Format for Academic Staff College

SOPQ: Which of the following has been evolved by you for the establishment of the Academic Staff College?	f	%
(a) ASC has been established as a separate entity within the University	24	100
(b) ASC has been established as a part of an existing department of continuing education.	00	N.A.
(c) ASC has been established as a wing of the College Development Council.	00	N.A.
(d) ASC has been established in the form of a State Institute of Educational Planning and Administration.	00	N.A.

N = 24

CHAPTER-IV

Course Content and Course Materials

In this Chapter the existing plan and policies pertaining to course content and course materials, personnel involved in the preparation of course materials, payment made to the course writers, distribution of course materials, suitability and quality of the course content and course materials, purpose served by and academic value of the orientation programmes have been surveyed. Thereafter, an attempt has been made to evaluate the entire system of course content and course materials in the light of the participant teachers' perception and theoretical thinking in this regard.

As regards the course content of the OPs, the UGC had developed a curriculum framework for the ASCs at the "National Workshop on Academic Staff Colleges" held at the university of Bombay on 14th August 1987. This workshop conceived the curriculum for the OPs of the ASCs to have the following four components.

(i) Component A: Awareness of linkages between Society, Environment, Development and Education.

(ii) Component B: Philosophy of Education, Indian Education System and Pedagogy.

(iii) Component C: Subject Up gradation.

(iv) Component D: Management and Personality Development.

Moreover, each component is consisted of different sub-topics. Despite the topics enlisted by the workshop under each of these components, many of the ASCs have made certain changes and incorporated topics according to their local needs and availability of resource persons. However, many questions were raised regarding the planning, structure, relevance and acceptance of the curriculum offered by the ASCs in India for the orientation of the university and college teachers. Thus, an empirical study of these aspects has been undertaken by the investigator so as to provide a purposeful curriculum for the OPs of the ASCs.

PLANNING OF THE COURSE CONTENT

An enquiry into the planning and execution of course content, the Directors and staffs of the ASCs revealed that most of the ASCs, i.e. 91.17% strictly follow the UGC guidelines in regard to the course content of the OPs (see the result in Table 4.1). Only 8.83% respondents stated that they do not follow the UGC guidelines. Responding to an open question, 8 83% staff stated that they were inspired to bring changes in the course content of the OPs: (a) according to the needs and nature of the participants, (b) as it is difficult to get reputed resource persons, (c) for maintaining uniformity of the course content with other ASCs, and (d) for making the programme more relevant to the needs of the society.

Moreover, the staffs of ASCs were asked to give their opinion to a question as to: who should plan the course content? There were four possible responses. The results in Table 4.1 indicate that in 79.17% cases, respective authority of the ASCs should plan the course content, in 37.5% cases, UGC should plan it. Similarly, 45.83% and 4.17% staffs are of the opinion that subject experts and university concerned should plan the course content of the OPs, respectively.

Table -4.1: Planning the Course Content

SOPQ: Do you follow strictly the UGC guidelines as regards course content?		f	%
	Yes	22	91.17
	No	02	8.83
SOPQ: In your opinion, who should plan the course content?			
(a)	Respective authority of the ASC.	19	79.17
(b)	UGC	09	37.50
(c)	Subject Experts	11	45.83
(d)	University	01	4.17

N = 24, but multiple responses possible

STRUCTURE OF THE COURSE CONTENT

As regards the structure of the course content of the OPs, majority of the staff, i.e. 70.83% of the ASCs observed that it is necessary to maintain uniformity in the structure of course content of various ASCs (see Table 4.2). Moreover, they suggested that this uniformity could be achieved:

(i) by regular meetings, discussions, etc. by Directors of ASCs; and

(ii) through Standing Committee of the ASCs or by following UGC guidelines.

On the other hand, 29 17% staff stated that it is not necessary to maintain uniformity in the structure of course content of various ASCs.

The results in the same Table 4.2 also reveal the different areas of the course content offered in the OPs. In 91.67% cases, the course content offered by the ASCs involves different aspects of teaching and administration; most of the staff, i.e. 95.83%

observe that different aspects of higher education and professional role of the teachers are included in the course content; 58.33% observe that latest trends in teachers, own discipline were included in the course content; and 83.33% staff stated that the course content offered by the ASCs involve organisation and management of higher education. Besides these four aspects, the respondents also suggested some additional areas such as; (i) civic responsibility of the citizen, (ii) management and personality development, (iii) monitoring and evaluation, and (iv) human rights, environmental education, women studies, library, physical education, yoga to be included in the course content offered by the ASCs in India.

Table - 4.2: Structure of the Course Content

SOPQ. Is it necessary to maintain uniformity in the structure of course content of various ASCs?		f	%
	Yes	17	70.83
	No	07	29.17
SOPQ: The course content offered by your ASC involves.			
(a) Different aspects of teaching and administration.		22	91.67
(b) Different aspects of higher education and professional role of teachers.		23	95.83
(c) Latest trends in teachers own discipline.		14	58.33
(d) Organisation and management of higher education		20	83.33

N= 24, but multiple responses possible

COURSE COMPONENTS

The staffs of the ASCs were asked a question pertaining to the fulfillment of attaining the aims of university education through four course components devised by the UGC. The results in Table 4.3 show that almost all the respondents, i.e. 95.83% thought that the four course components devised by the UGC fulfill the attainment of aims of university education, while only 4.17% respondents did not think the same. To them (4.17%), the course components of the OPs could be meaningful if: (i) subject up gradation (Component C) would be deleted, and (ii) course component on Information Technology and Computer Application would be added.

The results in Table 4.3 also show the ranks assigned to the four course components as given by the staffs of ASCs. The staffs were asked to give a rank (1,2,3,4 etc.) to each of the four components according to the emphasis given. Rank 1 indicates foremost emphasis and rank 4 indicates least emphasis. A score of 4 was given to rank 1, and a score of 1 was given to rank 4. Similarly, rank 2 and 3 were scored as 3 and 2, respectively. The frequency of each rank was multiplied by the respective rank score and summation of these score gave the total rank score for each course component. Accordingly, ranks were found on the basis of rank scores as presented in the Table 3. From the results it is observed that Component 'A', i.e. awareness of linkages between Society, Environment, Development and Education is placed on rank 1 with rank score 69; Philosophy of Education, Indian System and Pedagogy, i.e. Component 'B' is placed on rank 2 with 47 score; rank 3 is Management and Personality Development, (Component 'D') and Component 'C', i.e. Subject up gradation is placed on rank 4 with the rank score 37 by the ASCs. Thus, it is worth noting that subject up gradation (Component C) is least emphasized by the ASCs in India.

Table - 4.3: Course Components and their Ranks

SOPQ: Do you think that the four course components devised by the UGC fulfill the attainment of aims of university education?		f	%
	Yes	23	95.83
	No	01	4.17
SOPQ: The course content for the general OPs suggested by the UGC consists of the following four components. Please rank order (1,2,3,4 etc.) these components in the list below according to the emphasis given at your institution.		Rank	Rank score
(a) Awareness of linkages between Society, Environment, Development and Education		1	69
(b) Philosophy of Education, Indian Education System and Pedagogy		2	47
(c) Subject Up gradation		4	37
(d) Management and Personality Development		3	46

N = 24

ACCEPTANCE OF THE COURSE CONTENT

As far as receiving of course content by the participants through the perception of the staff of the ASCs, the results in Table 4.4 indicate that almost all the staffs, i.e. 95.83% of the ASCs think that the present course content of the orientation course is well received by the participants. Only 4.17% staffs think that it is not well received by the participants.

They (4.17%) suggest that inter-disciplinary approach of the subject should be included at Master-degree level, and course content of the ASC should be made available to the aspirant teachers who want to get them oriented.

Table - 4.4; Acceptance of the Course Content

SOPQ: Do you think that the present course content of the orientation programme has been well received by the participants?		f	%
	Yes	23	95.83
	No	01	4.17

N = 24

CONSTITUTION OF COURSE MATERIALS

With respect to the constitution of course materials for the OPs of the ASCs in India, the results in Table 4.5 show that the course materials of majority of the ASCs, i.e. 54.17% constitute of booklets consisting of reading materials; whereas every third ASCs, i.e. 33.33% use a package of reading materials and audio tapes. Similarly, out of 24 respondents, 37.5% have revealed that the course materials for a typical course offered at the ASCs constitute of a package of reading materials and audio-video tapes. Moreover, almost all the ASCs. i.e. 95.83% offer course materials in the form of lecture handouts/synopsis written by resource persons; while the course materials of every two of the three ASCs, i.e. 66.67% constitute printed books and materials. Similarly, 70.83% respondents state that optimum use of the library facilities of the ASCs are offered for a typical course; only 20.83%, i.e. approximately every fifth of the ASCs constitute of documentation section for the ready reference of the course materials; and every sixth of the ASCs, i.e. 16.67% offer ASC News Letter. Local college libraries are made available by 45.83% ASCs as regards to the course materials for a typical orientation course in India.

Table - 4.5: Constitution of Course Materials

SOPQ: What constitutes the materials for a typical course offered at your Institution?	f	%
(a) Booklets consisting of reading materials.	13	54.17
(b) A package of reading materials and audiotapes.	08	33.33
(c) A package of reading materials and audio-video tapes.	09	37.50
(d) Lecture handouts/synopsis written by Resource Persons.	23	95.83
(e) Printed books and materials.	16	66.67
(f) Optimum use of library facilities of the ASCs.	17	70.83
(g) Documentation section for the ready reference.	05	20.83
(h) Academic Staff College News Letter.	04	16.67
(i) Local College libraries are made available.	11	45.83

N = 24, but multiple responses possible,

PREPARATION OF COURSE MATERIALS

Writing and preparation of course materials is an important task of the OPs of the ASCs. Different models have been adopted by the ASCs in developing course materials for the OPs. A significant system for the preparation and development of course materials is the 'Course Team' approach through which a team consisting of renowned educationists, experts, specialists with high academic quality are engaged in developing course materials of the ASCs. Moreover, in some cases, internal staffs of the ASCs are involved in developing course materials and in other the resource persons themselves prepare the course materials of the OPs. Despite these facts, the investigator felt the importance of undertaking an empirical study to ascertain the nature and procedure of preparation of course materials of the OPs of the ASCs in India. Thus, in the present study, an attempt has been made to study the nature and procedure of the preparation of course materials of the OPs in respect of the personnel involved - internal staff/outside experts, payment to the outside experts, procedure of involving outside experts, and distribution of course materials, etc.

PERSONNEL INVOLVED

The Directors and staff of ASCs were asked a question as to who develops the course materials for different course components? There were four possible responses. The results of the study (Table 4.6) reveal that in 45.83% cases, the core staff of the ASCs develop the course materials for different course components; in 54.17% cases, the course materials are developed by the outside subject experts; both staff and the outside subject experts are involved in the preparation of most of the course materials, i.e. 70.83%; while every third ASCs (33.33%) use course materials prepared by some other institutions.

Table - 4.6: Personnel Involved in the Preparation of Course Materials

SOPQ: Who develops the course materials for different course components offered in your institution?	f	%
(a) The core staff of the ASC.	11	45.83
(b) The outside subject experts.	13	54.17
(c) Both staff and the outside subject experts.	17	70.83
(d) Use of the course materials prepared by some other institutions.	08	33.33

N = 24, but multiple responses possible.

INTERNAL STAFF

As 45.83% (Table 4.6) course materials are prepared by the core staff of the ASCs, a logical query was made about the nature of their involvement in the preparation of course materials. The results in Table 4.7 indicate that in 12.50% cases (out of 45.83%), the course materials are developed by the internal subject specialist course coordinators of the ASCs. In 25% cases, the materials are prepared by a group of subject specialist coordinators; and in 8.33% cases, a course team (subject specialist and media experts) are involved in writing the course materials for the OPs of the ASCs in India. Besides these, the respondents also state that the Directors of the ASCs are also involved in developing course materials for the different course components of the OPs.

Table - 4.7: Involvement of Internal Staffs in the Preparation of Course Materials

SOPQ: If the staffs of your institutions develop the course materials, then which of the following applies to you?	f	%
(a) Subject specialist course coordinators alone.	03	12.50
(b) A group of subject specialist coordinators alone.	06	25.00
(c) A course team (subject specialist and media experts).	02	08.33

N = 24

OUTSIDE EXPERTS

As regards the involvement of the subject experts in developing course materials, it is seen in Table 4.6 that 54.17% course materials are developed by outside experts. In this section, an attempt has been made to find out as to who are these outside experts and with what background they are involved in developing course materials.

The results in Table 4.8 indicate that every sixth, i.e. 16.67% outside experts involved in preparing course materials are subject specialists. Only 4.17% outside experts are both subject and media experts who develop course materials of the OPs. But, every third of the outside experts, i.e. 33.33% engaged in developing course materials are experienced teachers of the subject speciality. It is therefore, clear that no media experts are engaged in developing course materials. Furthermore, RPs are also involved in developing course materials of the OPs.

Table - 4.8: Involvement of Outside Experts in Preparing Course Materials

SOPQ: If outside experts are asked to write course materials then are these experts:	f	%
(a) Subject specialists?	04	16.67
(b) Media experts?	N.A.	N.A.
(c) Both subject and media experts?	01	04.17
(d) Experienced teachers of the subject specialist?	08	33.33

N = 24

PAYMENT TO THE OUTSIDE COURSE WRITERS

The staffs of the ASCs were asked a question as: do they pay to the outside course writers? The results in Table 4.9 show that every sixth, i.e. 16.67% ASCs pay outside course writers for preparing lecture notes while two of the every three ASCs, i.e. 66.67% do not pay the outside course writers. However, 16.67% staffs of the ASCs remain silent in this regard. The next question of the questionnaire was asked to those staff of the ASCs who responded that outside course writers are paid for preparing lecture notes (16.67% in Table 4.9). They were asked as to how much money for individual lecture note is paid to the outside course writers? Accordingly, it is found that the outside course writers are paid Rs. 400/- for preparing lecture notes for the OPs.

Table - 4.9: Payment to the Outside Course Writers for Preparing Lecture Notes

SOPQ: Do you pay to the outside course writers for preparing lecture notes?		f	%
	Yes	04	16.67
	No	16	66.67
	No Response	04	16.67

N = 24

PROCEDURE FOR ASKING OUTSIDE EXPERTS TO WRITE COURSE MATERIALS

An enquiry into the procedures adopted for asking outside experts to write course materials of the OPs, reveals that (a) in 33.33% cases, the selected topics of a particular OP are sent to the outside experts and they are asked to write the course materials; and (b) in 16.67% cases, an instructional manual is sent to the experts along with the selected topics to write the course materials. Besides these, the staffs also stated that (i) an invitation is extended to all the eminent scholars to select and write the topics according to their specialties, and (ii) resource persons are requested to prepare synopsis notes for the topics of their lectures.

Table - 4.10: Procedure for Asking Outside Experts to Write the Course Materials

SOPQ: What is the procedure for asking the outside experts to write the course materials?	f	%
(a) They are sent the selected topics of a particular OP and are asked to write the course materials.	08	33.33
(b) An instructional manual is sent to the experts along with the selected topics.	04	16.67

N = 24

DISTRIBUTION OF COURSE MATERIALS

As regards the distribution of course materials of the OPs, the results (Table 4.11) indicate that in case of 16.67%, the course materials developed for the participants of a particular course are distributed at the beginning of the course; in 20.83% cases, course materials are distributed at the end of the course; and in most of the cases (62.50%), the course materials developed for the participants of the OPs are distributed during the course.

Table - 4.11: Distribution of Course Materials

SOPQ: The course materials developed for the participants of a particular course are distributed:	f	%
(a) At the beginning of the course.	04	16.67
(b) At the end of the course.	05	20.83
(c) During the course.	15	62.50

N = 24

SUITABILITY OF THE COURSE CONTENT AND COURSE MATERIALS

As the participants are the sole receiving agents and real users of the course content and course materials offered by the ASCs, their opinions about the suitability of the course content and course materials is of extreme importance. Nobody else than the teacher participants can tell about the effectiveness of the course content and course materials, which are offered to them during the OP. Thus, in this section, an attempt has been made to study the effectiveness of course content and course materials of the OPs through the perception of the teacher participants.

PARTICIPANTS' PERCEPTION OF WEIGHTAGE TO COURSE COMPONENT

Perception of participants pertaining to the percentage of emphasis given to each course component of the OPs, in Table 4.12 show that participants found almost equal emphasis to all the course components. But a close observation of the results reveal that ranging from 10% to 85%, participants gave an average 30.48% importance to the component 'A' (Linkages between Society, Environment, Development and Education). Similarly, 30.11% (ranging from 10% to 75%) emphasis was given to component 'B' (Philosophy of Education, Indian Education System and Pedagogy); on an average the highest 31.95% (ranging from 10% to 80%) emphasis was given to component 'C' (Subject up gradation); and ranging from 10% to 90%, on an average 31.49% emphasis was given to component 'D' (Management and Personality Development) in the OPs of the ASCs in India.

Furthermore, a comparative observation between Table 4.3 and Table 4.12 regarding course component show that (a) the staff of the ASCs give highest rank to the component 'A', whereas the participants perceive the same at the third place; (b) component 'B' is ranked 2 by the staff, whereas participants assign least percentage of emphasis to it; (c) the staff give lowest rank to the component 'C, whereas the participants give it the highest weightage; and (d) the component 'D' is ranked 3 by the staff of the ASCs, whereas the participants perceive the same at the third place.

The discrepancy between the motives of the ASCs and-perception of the participants, as revealed in the results, relating to the weightage given to each course component of the OPs indicate that the ASCs attempt to give more emphasis to component 'A' and "B', but participants who are the real beneficiaries find the component 'C and 'D' as more suitable.

Thus, it is hypothesized that in component 'C and component 'D'. (i) the resource persons might have shown better knowledge of the subject, presentation and interaction with the participants; (ii) the course content might be more relevant and up to date; (iii) the course materials might be more interesting, motivating and sufficient; and (iv) more interesting and effective media might have been incorporated with the course content than the component 'A' and 'B' of the OPs.

Table - 4.12: Perception of the Participants Pertaining to the Weightage given to each Course Component

PFQ: Below are given four course components of the OPs as suggested by the UGC. Please give percentage of emphasis given to each component in the OPs	Range of %	Average %
(a) Component' A' (Linkages between Society, Environment, Development and Education)	10-85	30.48
(b) Component 'B' (Philosophy of Education, Indian Education System and Pedagogy)	10 - 75	30.11
(c) Component 'C' (Subject Up gradation)	10-80	31.95
(d) Component 'D' (Management and Personality Development)	10 - 90	31.49

N = 765

QUALITIES OF THE COURSE CONTENT AND COURSE MATERIALS

The participants were asked to respond a question in which five qualities, considered essential for an effective course content and course materials, were presented; and they were asked to tick mark if the quality in question was always, sometimes or never present in the course content and course materials offered to them.

The results presented in Table 13 reveal that on the whole, almost every third (34.30%) teacher participants find all five qualities in the course content and course materials of the OPs. However, there are two exceptions to this: (a) 29.54% participants do not find the presentation of course content always interesting; and (b) every fourth (25 49%) participants do not find supplied course materials of a high academic standard.

Moreover, it is observed that sometimes 52.16% participants find all the five essential qualities in the course content and course materials. It is also found that (i) 51.37% ASCs sometimes provide course materials to the participants; (ii) every second (50.07%) participants sometimes find the offered course contents of academic standard; (iii) in 62.88% cases, participants sometimes find the presentation of the course content interesting; (iv) equal to the overall percentage, i.e. 52.16% participants sometimes find the supplied course materials of a high academic standard; (v) only 44.31% participants sometimes observe that the course materials enable them to understand the concepts taught to them.

It appears that on the whole, 9.39% participants never find all the qualities in the course content and course materials of the OPs. 9.15% ASCs never provide course materials to the participants; 5.88%, 4.97% and 17.12% participants never find the course contents of academic standard, the presentation of the course contents interesting, supplied course materials of a high academic standard, respectively. And in 9.80% cases the course materials never enable the participants to understand the concepts taught through them. Moreover, overall 4.16% participants are reluctant to respond the question. Thus, it implies that about 15% of the course content and course materials on the whole lack all the five qualities as mentioned in Table 4.13.

Table - 4.13: Quality of the Course Content and Course Materials

PFQ: Qualities in question		Always		Sometimes		Never		No Response	
		f	%	f	%	f	%	f	%
(a)	Does your staff college provide course materials to you?	282	36.86	393	51.37	70	9.15	20	3.40
(b)	Do you find the offered course contents of acauemic standard?	311	40.65	383	50.07	45	5.88	26	3.40
(c)	Do you find the presentation of the course content interesting?	226	29.54	481	62.88	38	4.97	20	2.61
(d)	Do you find the supplied course materials of a high academic standard?	195	25.49	399	52.16	131	17.12	40	5.23
(e)	Do the course materials enable you to understand the concepts intended to/taught through them?	298	38.95	339	44.31	75	980	53	6.93
	Total (N = 765 X 5 = 3825)	321	34.30	1995	52.16	359	9.39	159	4.16

SUITABILITY OF THE COURSE MATERIALS

The participants of the OPs were asked to respond a question about the adequacy of the course materials supplied to them. There are four possible responses in the form of a scale.

The results given in Table 4.14 reveal that only 37.39% course materials are sufficient as perceived by the participants; in 46.14% cases, the course materials supplied to the participants are not so sufficient; and in 12.94% cases, course materials supplied are not at all sufficient. Moreover, 3.53% participants do not respond the question. Thus, it is discouraging to observe that most of the course materials supplied to the participants in the OPs are not sufficient.

In the next question of the questionnaire, the participants were asked as "on the whole, are you satisfied with course materials supplied to you?" The results in Table 4.14 indicate that majority of the participants (61.83%) of the OPs are satisfied with course materials supplied to them, while 34.77% participants are not satisfied with the same. Moreover, 3.40% participants do not respond the question. Thus, it is concluded that most of the course materials supplied are not up to the mark. But it is difficult to say if the absence of the above five qualities is the cause of dissatisfaction. Thus, an open-ended question was asked to all those participants who reported dissatisfaction with the course materials; they had to mention what dissatisfied them.

Table - 4.14: Suitability of the Course Materials

PFQ The course materials supplied to you are -		f	%
	Sufficient	286	37.39
	Not so sufficient	353	46.14
	Not at all sufficient	99	12.94
	No response	27	3.53
PFQ: On the whole, are you satisfied with course materials supplied to you?			
	Yes	473	61.83
	No	266	34.77
	No response	26	3.40

N = 765

The participants enlisted a variety of causes relating to course materials, which dissatisfied them. A few very relevant and the most frequently mentioned causes are reported below:

(a) Course materials supplied are obsolete, irrelevant, and lack clarity.

(b) Books are not provided.

(c) Course materials are repeated from one course to another.

(d) Course materials provided are incomplete and are not scientifically prepared.

(e) Course materials are supplied late.

(f) No course materials are provided on research methodology, examination and evaluation, teaching methodology, motivation and personality development.

PURPOSES SERVED BY THE ORIENTATION PROGRAMMES

We will get a better picture of the purposes served by the orientation programmes later when we examine the perception of the participants, as they are the real beneficiaries of these orientation programmes. However, it is worth noting the purpose perceived to be served by the staff of the ASCs through their orientation programmes. It is with this intention, a list of nine possible purposes that could be served during the orientation pragrammes were placed before the staff that actually involved in the orientation programmes. These staff members were asked to put a tick mark against the purposes they perceived to be served during the orientation pragrammes and give ranks one, two, three etc. to each according to the extent it was served. Rank one indicated the foremost purpose served and rank nine indicated the least purpose served. A score of nine was given to rank one and a score of one to nine. The other ranks were scored in between as eight, seven, six, five... etc., for ranks two, three, four, five, etc. respectively. The frequency of each rank was multiplied by the respective rank score and a summation of these gave a total rank score of each purpose served. Accordingly, ranks were found on the basis of rank scores. Table -4.15 presents the results of this analysis.

A reference to the rank scores in Table - 4.15 indicates that the foremost purpose served during the orientation programmes is that the excellence in the academic standards of the university and college teachers is promoted. Teachers' acquaintahce with the recent innovations in the area of teaching and pedagogical science comes at the second place. The purpose perceived to be served at the third and fourth places are indicative of the staffs, concern for ensuring teachers' professional growth and creating awareness among them about the society and environment in which they live. An important purpose of relating education with national development is seen to be served at the fifth place. The sixth and seventh purposes served are quite in the expectations of the University Education Commission (1948 - 49) and the University Grants Commission. However, it is seen that the eighth and ninth purpose, i.e., to disseminate knowledge and service to the society and to upgrade teachers' knowledge about the respective subjects perceived to be achieved by the staffs of the ASCs during the orientation programmes.

Table- 4.15: Purposes served by the Orientation Programmes as Perceived by the Staffs

Q: Which of the following purposes are served by the Orientation Programme at your ASC?	Rank	Rank Score
1. Excellence in academic standards is promoted	1	100
2. Teachers' professional growth is ensured	4	81
3. Awareness among the teachers about the society and environment is created	3	83
4. Teachers are encouraged to relate education with national development	5	76
5. Teachers are motivated to evolve a philosophy of education	7	55
6. Teachers are acquainted with the recent innovations in the area of teaching and pedagogical sciences	2	91
7. Optimum growth of teachers personality is ensured	6	68
8. Knowledge of the teachers about the respective subject is upgraded	9	48
9. Dissemination of knowledge and service to the society takes place	8	49

N = 24

ACADEMIC VALUE OF ORIENTATION PROGRAMMES

As the university and college teachers are the main beneficiaries of the orientation programmes, their opinion as to what they think of the academic Value of orientation programmes is of extreme importance. No body other than the teachers can tell whether the orientation programmes are beneficial for their profession. In fact, teachers' attitude towards the orientation programmes has been taken as a criterion to judge the suitability of the orientation programmes in this study. They were also asked specified questions with a view to improving the quality and suitability of the orientation programmes. This section, thus, evaluates the academic value of the orientation programmes offered by various ASCs in the light of the feedback received from the teachers.

The teachers were asked to respond to a question in which eleven academic values, considered essential for an effective orientation programme, were presented; they were asked to tick mark if the value in question was present in the orientation programmes offered to them by various ASCs. The frequencies with corresponding percentages, indicating the presence of each value as perceived by the teachers, are presented in Table -4.16.

The overall percentage in Table - 4.16 reveals that on the whole almost all the participants find all the eleven academic values beneficial for them. It is also seen in Table - 4.16 that as many as 88.63% of the teachers report that they benefited after undergoing the orientation programmes in terms of identifying and developing effective style of teaching, whereas as low as 51.76% of the teachers opine that orientation programmes are beneficial to them in terms of knowing and playing one's role effectively.

However, it is worth mentioning that a good majority of teachers find the orientation programmes to be of high academic value in terms of: (a) imparting knowledge effectively (85.75%); (b) making proper choice of teaching method (82.22%); (c) linking research with the task of developing effective methodology of teaching (73.20%); (d) planning and executing teaching properly and confidently (78.43%); .(e) preparing and using teaching aids effectively (74.34%); (f) organizing different co-curricular activities (67.97%); (g) developing and understanding the system and role of higher education (77.91%); (h) developing participating skills and management techniques (77.25%); and acquiring the latest knowledge and skills (72.68%).

The overall percentages in Table — 4.16 reveal that on the whole almost all (69.23 percent) teachers find all the eleven academic values present in the orientation programmes attended by them.

Table-4.16: Academic Values of Orientation Programmes

Q. Which of the following benefits do you get after undergoing orientation programmes?	f	%
1. Identify and develop effective style of teaching	678	88.63
2. Impart knowledge effectively	656	85.75
3. Make a proper choice of the teaching method as the situation demands	629	82.22
4. Link research with the task of developing an effective methodology of teaching	560	73.20
5. Plan and execute daily teaching lessons properly and confidently	600	78.43
6. Prepare required teaching aids and use them effectively	584	76.34
7. Organize different co-curricular activities	520	67.97
8. Develop a comprehensive understanding of the system and role of higher education	596	77.91
9. Develop participating skills and management techniques	591	77.25
10. Acquire a lot of latest knowledge and skills	556	72.68
11. Know and play one's role effectively	396	51.76
Total (N=765x 11 =8415)	5826	69.23

SUGGESTIONS

The next two questions in the questionnaire invited suggestions from the participants for improving the quality of the course content and course materials of the OPs. The participants made several suggestions including eliminating the overlapping and irrelevant ones, which are reported below:

On the basis of frequency of mentioning, following areas have been found more relevant for university/college teachers to be included in the course content of the orientation programmes: (a) information technology; (b) teaching techniques; (c) socio-economic and political conditions of India; (d) value education; (e) research methodology and the priority areas of research study; (f) class-room management; (g) teachers' rights and obligations; and (h) crisis in present education system and higher education. Moreover course content should be made up to-date, relevant and research oriented.

As regards the course materials of the OPs, the most frequently listed suggestions by the participants are:

(i) Lecture handouts should be supplied,

(ii) The course materials should be up to date, relevant and should cover entire course content,

(iii) The course materials should be provided well in advance and in time,

(iv) Books and journals should be provided,

(v) Discussions on materials should be held in the session and should be illustrated with plenty of examples,

(vi) Research reference materials should be given.

CHAPTER-V

ORGANISATION, ADMINISTRATION AND DURATION

This Chapter begins with the issue whether participation in OPs be compulsory or voluntary. Thus, it was thought appropriate to know from the teacher participants the present conditions for participation in OPs and to study their desires if they would like the participation to be made compulsory or voluntary. Thereafter, this Chapter addresses to some more questions like, of what value is the OPs to the participants? Do they really mean what they claim to be? What actually goes on during the OPs? Is the OP organized by the ASCs full time and residential? What constitutes the core staff and is it essential to appoint a standing committee for the organisation of the ASCs? Lastly, are the OPs worth the time and money spent to attend them?

NUMBER OF ORIENTATION COURSES ORGANISED IN ONE YEAR

An enquiry into the number of orientation courses organized by the ASCs in one academic year reveals that only 8.33% of the respondents reported of organizing three orientation courses in one year; half of them (50% presented in Table 5.1) organize four orientation courses; 16.67% respondents reported of organizing five orientation courses and every fourth (25%) of them reported that six orientation courses are organized by their ASCs in one year. The details results of the analysis are presented in Table 5.1.

Table - 5.1: Number of Orientation Courses organized by the ASCs in one year

SOPQ: How many orientation courses are organized by your institution in one year?	f	%
(a) 3 Orientation Courses	02	8.33
(b) 4 Orientation Courses	12	50.00
(c) 5 Orientation Courses	04	16.67
(d) 6 Orientation Courses	06	25.00

N = 24

COMPULSORY/ VOLUNTARY PARTICIPATION IN ORIENTATION PROGRAMMES

The issue whether participation in orientation programmes be compulsory or voluntary in ASCs is still unresolved. Hence, it was thought appropriate to know from the university and college teachers the present condition laid down by their ASCs for participation in orientation programmes. Further, an attempt was made to study their desires if they would like the participation in orientation programmes to be made compulsory or voluntary.

The results in Table - 5.2 indicate that 70.33% teachers want participation in orientation programmes to be made compulsory. This in itself is an indicator of the fact that orientation programmes are viewed very positively by a majority of the teachers. It appears that the staff of the ASCs ensured teachers' cognitive involvement in the orientation programmes. Hence, the general notion that university and college teachers being adults and having already acquired master degree and above would not like to be guided and governed by others and therefore do not prefer control (say in the form of compulsion to participate in orientation programmes) does not apply to university and college teachers who received orientation programmes in the ASCs In India. The probable reasons for this are that the participants have been able to receive a comprehensive understanding of our system and various other dimensions and inter-linkages which might have enhanced their teaching skills, participating abilities and the management techniques. However, it appears that only 29.41% university and college teachers want participation in orientation programmes to be made voluntary, whereas only 0.26% teachers remain neutral in this regard. Whatever may be the reasons, this is an important area for research, as it has important implications for deciding whether participation in orientation programmes should be compulsory or voluntary. Preferably/it could be compulsory, as a good majority of teachers want that.

Table - 5.2: Compulsory/Voluntary Participation in Orientation Programmes.

Questions	Compulsory		Voluntary		No Response	
	f	%	f	%	f	%
Q. 1. Is the participation in Orientation Programmes compulsory or voluntary in the ASCs?	675	88.24	87	11.37	03	0.39
Q.2. In your opinion, should the participation in Orientation Programmes be compulsory or voluntary?	538	70.33	225	29.41	02	0.26

N = 765

SUITABILITY OF THE ORIENTATION PROGRAMMES

Suitability of the orientation programmes in this study implies the suitability of the venue, the time and the activities that are organized. The responses to these questions are analyzed and presented in Table-5.3 and 5.4. From the results shown in Table 5.3, it is clear that the venue of orientation programmes suits 88.24% of the participants and it does not suit 10.33%, whereas 1.43% of the participants do not give response in this regard. Similarly, in the case of 82.61% the orientation programmes are organized during the time when they really need them, but this is not the case for 15.43% of the participants, whereas 1.96% of the participants remain silent in this regard. Thus, in general, it appears that the organisation of orientation programmes suits a good majority of participants.

Nonetheless, it does not suit a very limited number of participants. Who are those participants? This is an important question for further research, as its empirical answer will provide the basis for organizing orientation programmes that will suit these participants.

Table - 5.3: Suitability of Orientation Programmes

Questions		Compulsory		Voluntary		No Response	
		f	%	f	%	f	%
Q.1	Are the Orientation Programmes organized at places that suit you?	675	88.24	79	10.33	11	1.43
Q-2	Are the Orientation Programmes organized during the time when you need them?	632	82.61	118	15.43	15	1.96

N = 765

Further, the suitability of the orientation programmes in terms of the activities that are organized has been ascertained under four different parameters. The Table - 5.4 presents the details of analysis done in this respect.

As regards the suitability of the activities during the orientation programmes, 63.53% of the participants perceive the same adequate, whereas 29.54% and 5.49% of the participants perceive orientation programmes less adequate and not adequate, respectively. However, only 1 44% of the participants do not give response in this regard.

Similarly, 65.36% of participants are satisfied with the quality of the organized activities of the orientation programmes as they feel them up-to-date and only 28.24% and 4.44% of participants feel these activities not up-to-date and obsolete, respectively. However, only 1.96% of the participants are having no response in this respect.

With regard to the relevance of the organized activities, 25.36% and 66.93% of the participants perceive them most relevant and relevant, respectively and only 6.41% find them irrelevant. However, merely 1.30% participants remain neutral in this regard.

Moreover, in the case of 58.82% of the participants the communication of the orientation programmes is perceived to be very effective and the same is not so effective in the case of only 38. 69%. Similarly, in the case of 1.57% the orientation programmes are not at all effective, and merely 0.92% remain silent on this issue.

Thus, it appears that the orientation programmes in general, offered by various ASCs in India suit a good majority of university and college teachers.

Table - 5.4: Suitability of Orientation Programmes

Questions		f	%
Q. 1 Are the Orientation Programmes attended by you:	Adequate	486	63.53
	Less Adequate	226	29.54
	Not Adequate	42	5.49
	No Response	11	1.44
Q.2. Is the quality of Orientation Programmes:	Up-to-date	500	65.36
	Not up-to-date	216	28.24
	Obsolete	34	4.44
	No Response	15	1.96
Q.3. Is the relevance of Orientation Programmes:	Most Relevant	194	25.36
	Relevant	512	66.93
	Irrelevant	49	6.41
	No Response	10	1.30
Q.4. Is the communication of Orientation Programmes:	Very Effective	450	58.82
	Not So Effective	296	38.69
	Not at all Effective	12	1.57
	No Response	07	0.92

N = 765

DURATION OF ORIENTATION COURSE

As regards duration of orientation course in one module, the staffs involved in the ASCs were asked to respond a question 'what is the average duration of the course in one module?' The question was open-ended, but the responses given by the staff of the ASCs were made into three groups in terms of duration (days) conveniently. The results presented in Table - 5.5 indicate that only 4.17% respondents (out of total 24) report that the average duration of the course in one module is 21 days. Almost all of them, i.e. 91.66% reveal that average duration is 28 days; and only 4.17% reveal the same as 30 - 35 days. Thus, it is evident that the ASCs in India have invariably followed the UGC guidelines of 28 days orientation course The results of analysis are presented in Table - 5.5.

Table - 5.5: Average Duration of the Orientation Course

SOPQ: What is the average duration of the Orientation Course in one module?		f	%
(a)	21 days	01	4.17
(b)	28 days	22	91.66
(c)	30 - 35 days	01	4.17

N = 24

NATURE OF ORGANISATION OF ORIENTATION PROGRAMME

The responses of the staff of the ASCs to a question regarding the nature of organisation of the OPs show that all the respondents under investigation (100% shown in Table - 5.6) report that the OP organized by the ASCs is inter-disciplinary in nature. Moreover, the results shown in the Table - 5.6 also reveal that 8.83% respondents report of covering 4-5 disciplines at a time in one OP. Similarly, 20.83% of them reveal that 5-6 disciplines and 41.67% report that 6-7 disciplines/respectively are being offered by their colleges in one OP. It is interesting to note that as many as 29.17% respondents reveal that more than 7 disciplines are covered in the OP at a time. From the results it may be observed that most of the

ASCs invite participants from more than 5 disciplines for an OP at a time. It is encouraging to note that the OPs organized by various ASCs in India cover almost all the subjects taught in the Indian universities and colleges.

Table - 5.6: Nature of Organisation

SOPQ: The OP organized by your institution is-		f	%
-	Interdisciplinary	24	100
-	Subject Specific	00	N.A.
SOPQ: If interdisciplinary, then it represents			
(a)	4 -5 disciplines at a time	02	8.33
(b)	5-6 disciplines at a time	05	20.83
(c)	6 -7 disciplines at a time	10	41.83
(d)	More than 7 disciplines at a time	07	29.17

ACADEMIC ADVISORY COMMITTEE OF THE ASCs

The staffs involved in the ASCs were asked to respond a question 'Do you have an Academic Advisory Committee?' The results given in Table - 5.7 indicate that almost all the respondents, i.e. 95.83% (out of total 24) reveal that ASCs have an Academic Advisory Committee, while only 4.17% observe of having no such committee.

However, the staffs were also asked one more question pertaining to the role of the Academic Advisory Committee, and were provided with five possible roles of the Committee. The responses given in the same Table - 5.7 show that, (a) in case of 79.17% respondents the Academic Advisory Committee advises on the organisation of the orientation course; (b) selects resource persons in case of 33.33%; (c) in case of 41.67% the Committee advises on bringing new resource persons from time to time; (d) 79.17% reveal that it takes decision on the different aspects of the functioning of the ASCs; and (e) only 16.67% respondents observe that the role of the Committee is to give advice on the appointment and rotation of the course coordinators from module to module. Moreover, the respondents also state that the Academic Advisory Committee gives advice regarding the number of OPs to be conducted in a year on the basis of demand from teachers.

Table - 5.7: Academic Advisory Committee of the ASCs

SOPQ: Do you have an Academic Advisory Committee?		f	%
	Yes	23	95.83
	No	01	4.17
SOPQ: If yes, then which of the following roles the Advisory Committee plays?			
(a)	Advises on the organisation of the OP	19	79.17
(b)	Selects resource persons	08	33.33
(c)	Advises on bringing new resource persons from time to time	09	41.67
(d)	Takes decision on the different aspects of the functioning of the ASC	19	79.17
(e)	Gives advice on the appointment and rotation of the course coordinators from module to module	04	16.67

N = 24, but multiple responses possible

FULL TIME AND RESIDENTIAL

The responses of the staff involved in the ASCs regarding the organisation of orientation course show that majority of the respondents, i.e. 62.50% observe that orientation courses organized by the ASCs are full time and residential. Moreover, 50% are of the view that they maintain it throughout, while 12.50% reveal that they do not. Again, it is interesting to note that 37.50% respondents are of the view that orientation courses organized by the ASCs are not full time and residential. The results of analysis are presented in Table - 5.8.

Table - 5.8: Full time and Residential Organisation of the OPs

SOPQ: Is the Orientation Course organized by you full time and residential?		f	%
	Yes	15	62.50
	No	09	37.50
SOPQ: If yes, do you maintain it throughout?			
	Yes	12	50.00
	No	03	12.50

N = 24

METHODS OF ORGANISATION OF THE OPs

As regards the methods for organizing the OPs, the staffs of the ASCs were asked to respond three possible responses. The Table - 5.9 reveals that most of the respondents (91.67%) observe that the methods for organizing the orientation course come under the direct control of the Director of the ASCs. In case of 8.33% respondents, the methods for organizing the same rest with the co-operative efforts of the departments, while it does not rest with the part of an exiting department as revealed by the respondents. However, they were also asked to add any other methods besides those mentioned in the questionnaire, for organizing the OP. Responding to this open-ended item they mentioned that, (a) the Department of Education plays a crucial role in organizing the OPs; and (b) the ASC with the active involvement of course coordinators organizes the OPs.

Table - 5.9: Methods for Organizing OPs

SOPQ: The methods for organizing Orientation Courses involve:		f	%
(a)	Part of an existing departments	00	N.A.
(b)	Co-operative efforts of departments	02	08.33
(c)	Under the direct control of the Director of the ASC	22	91.67

N = 24

CORE STAFF OF ASCs

As regards the permanent core-staff, the staffs involved in the ASCs were asked to respond a question 'Do you have permanent core-staff?' The results given in Table - 5. 10 show that most of the respondents, i.e. 83.33% report that the ASCs have permanent core-staff, and only 16.67% of them observe of having no permanent core-staff.

Moreover, responding to a question regarding constitution of core-staff of the ASCs, the respondents state that they have one Director in each ASC (100%); one Reader (58.33%); Lecturer (50%); one Librarian (50%); Steno-Typist (75%); Peon (83.33%); Section Officer (37.5%); Senior Assistant (45.83%); Attendant (16.67%); Clerk (12.5%); Driver (4.17%); Helper (8.83%); and Watchman (8.83%), respectively.

However, an enquiry into the total number of core-staffs available in the ASCs, reveals that 149 core-staffs are there in 24 ASCs in India. It implies that about 6 (6.20) core-staffs, on an average, are there in each ASC.

Table-5.10: Core Staff of the ASCs in India

SOPQ: Do you have permanent core-staff?		f	%
	Yes	20	83
	No	04	16.67

SOPQ: If yes, what constitutes the core-staff of your institution				No. of core-staff		
	f	%	1	2	3	Total
(a) Director 24	100	24	-	24		
(b) Reader 14	58.33	14	-	14		
(c) Lecturer	12	50.00	10	02	-	14
(d) Librarian	12	50.00	12	-	-	12
(e) Steno Typist	18	75.00	13	05	-	23

(f) Peon	20	83.33	15	02	02	26
(g) Section Officer	09	37.50	09	-	-	09
(h) Senior Assistant	11	45.83	11	-	-	11
(i) Attendant	04	16.67	04	-	-	04
(j) Clerk	03	12.50	01	02	-	05
(k) Driver	01	4.17	01	-	-	01
(1) Helper	02	8.33	-	02	-	04
(m) Watchman	02	8.33	-	02	-	04
N = 24					Grand Total =	= 149

Average No. Of core-staff in each ASC (149/24) is 6 (6.20)

STANDING COMMITTEE

As regards the appointment of a Standing Committee; the staffs of the ASCs were asked to respond a question. The results presented in Table - 5.11 show that two of the every three respondents (66.67%) observe that it is essential to appoint a Standing Committee for the better organisation of the ASCs; whereas every third respondents (33.33%) believe that appointment of a Standing Committee is not essential.

Moreover, the respondents who were in favour of appointing a Standing Committee (66.67% in table -5.11) were asked one more question: 'If yes, who should appoint it?' The results shown in the same table - 5.11 reveal that 16.67% respondents are of the view that the UGC should appoint the Standing Committee, while only 4.17% observe that V.C. of the university should appoint it. Similarly, as high as 29.17% and as low as 16.67% reveal that it should be appointed by the university and ASC itself, respectively.

Table - 5.11: Standing Committee of the ASCs

SOPQ: Is it essential to appoint a Standing Committee for the better organisation of the ASCs?		f	%
	Yes	16	66.67
	No	08	33.33
SOPQ: If yes, who should appoint it?			
(a) UGC		04	16.67
(b) V.C.		01	4.17
(c) University		07	29.17
(d) ASC itself		04	16.67

N = 24

ORGANISATION OF SEMINAR/WORKSHOP/CONFERENCE

With an intention to study about the organisation of seminars/workshops/conferences, etc. for educational administrators, the responses of the staffs involved in the ASCs reveal that almost all the respondents, i.e. 95.83% in Table - 5.12 report that they organize seminars/workshops/conferences etc. for educational administrators and only 4.17% are of the opinion that their colleges do not hold such programmes. Moreover, they were also asked one more question pertaining to number of such programmes already organized by their ASCs. The results in Table - 5.12 reveal that 138 programmes have already been organized by ASCs, ranging from 1 to 17. The total number of programmes were divided by the number of respondents, and consequently, the number of programmes organized by each ASC is found to be 6 on an average. It implies that on an average, 6 programmes of seminars/workshops/conferences have been organized by an ASC for educational administrators.

Table - 5.12: Organisation of Seminar/Workshop/Conference for Administrators

SOPQ: Does your college organize workshops/ seminars/conferences, etc. for Educational Administrators?		f	%
	Yes	23	95.83
	No	01	4.17
SOPQ: How many programmes of Seminar/ Workshop/ Conference, etc. are organized by your ASC?	No. of Progs.	Range	Average Progs
	138	1-17	5.75

N = 24

INFRASTRUCTURE FACILITIES OF THE ASCs

With regard to the infrastructure facilities for organizing orientation programmes of the ASCs in India, the Directors were provided with a list of different facilities and were asked to respond to the facility if the ASC was equipped with. The results presented in the Table -5.13 show that 66.67% of ASCs in India have a separate and independent building while 33.33% do not have the same. It should be noted that all the ASCs (100%) in India are equipped with (a) library room, (b) room for Director and Staff, (c) T.V., (d) overhead projector, (e) type writer, and (f) telephone. Other facilities available in the ASCs are, (i) seminar room (75%); (ii) reading room (66.67%); (iii) hostel facility (41.67%); (iv) furniture for seminar and library (75%); (v) photocopier (75%); (vi) tape recorder (75%); (vii) VCR (83.33%); (viii) video-film camera (16.67%); (ix) AC/cooler (58.33%) and (x) computer (75%).

Moreover, the Directors of the ASCs were also asked to state if any other facilities were available in their ASCs besides those mentioned in the questionnaire. Very few of them mentioned that fax, e-mail and Internet, slide projector, printers, and generator machine were also available in one or other ASCs.

Table - 5.13: Infrastructure Facilities for Organizing OPs

SOPQ: Does your college equip with the following Infrastructure facilities?		Yes		No	
		f	%	f	%
(i)	A separate and independent building	08	66.67	04	33.33
(ii)	Seminar room	09	75.00	03	25.00
(iii)	Library room	12	100.00	00	N.A.
(iv)	Reading room	08*	66.67	04	33.33
(v)	Hostel facility	05	41.67	07	58.33
(vi)	Room for director and Staff	12	100.00	00	N.A.
(vii)	Furniture for seminar and library	09	75.00	03	25.00
(viii)	Photocopier	09	75.00	03	25:00
(ix)	T.V.	12	100.00	00	N.A.
(x)	Tape Recorder	09	75.00	03	25.00
(xi)	VCR	10	83.33	02	16.67
(xii)	Video-film camera	02	16.67	10	83.33
(xiii)	Overhead Projector	12	100.00	00	N.A.
(xiv)	Type writer	12	100.00	00	N.A.
(xv)	Telephone	12	100.00	00	N.A.
(xvi)	AC/cooler	07	58.33	05	41.67
(xvii)	Computer	09	75.00	03	25.00

N = 12 (Responses of Director of the sampled ASCs are considered)

SUITABILITY OF THE DURATION OF THE ORIENTATION PROGRAMME

As regards the suitability of the duration of the OPs, the perception of the participants have been analyzed and presented in Table - 5.14. From the results, it is observed that a good majority of teachers (78.95%) have perceived the present duration of 4 weeks OP quite sufficient. It is only in 20.52% cases, the same has not been found to be sufficient; and barely 0.53% is silent on this issue.

Moreover, the next question was asked to those participants who indicated that the present duration of 4 weeks of OPs was not sufficient. The results reveal that out of 20.52% (Table - 5.14), 10.98 have suggested that duration of the OP should be 1 to 3 weeks. Similarly, 4.44%. 3.53%, 0.92% and 0.65% have suggested for 7 to 8 weeks, 5 to 6 weeks, 11 to 12 weeks and 9 to 10 weeks duration, respectively.

Table - 5.14: Suitability of Duration of the OPs

PFQ: Do you feel that present duration of 4 weeks of OPs is quite sufficient?		f	%
	Yes	605	78.95
	No	157	20.52
	No Response	03	0.53
PFQ: If not, please suggest duration, which you feel proper.			
(a)	1-3 weeks	83	10.98
(b)	5 - 6 weeks	27	3.53
(c)	7 - 8 weeks	34	4.44
(d)	9-10 weeks	05	0.65
(e)	11 -12 weeks	07	0.92

N = 765

DAILY WORKING HOURS OF A TEACHER

The participants' opinion was sought regarding the daily working hours of a teacher. Table - 5.15 presents detail analysis of the responses. From the results, it is observed that a teacher should work about 5 hours (4.79) daily on an average as opined by the respondents. In order to find out the average hours, the mid-points of each class interval (in the column 'hours' in Table - 5.15) were multiplied by the frequency of mentioning, respectively and then, summation of the products was divided by total number of respondents (N).

Further, the responses of the participants were classified into six groups for the detailed analysis of the same. It is worthwhile to note participants' opinion that the daily working hours for a teacher should be; (a) 11 to 12 hrs. in case of 0.26%; (b) 9 to 10 hrs. in case of 2.48%; (c) 7 to 8 hrs. in case of 10.07%; (d) 5 to 6 hrs. in case of 47.97%; (e) 3 to 4 hrs. in case of 27.06%; and (f) 1 to 2 hrs in case of 12.16% participants, respectively.

Table - 5.15: Daily Working Hours of a Teacher

PFQ: How many clock hours a teacher should work daily to realize the objectives of the course?	Hours	f	%
	11-12	02	0.26
	9-10	19	2.48
	7-8	77	10.07
	5-6	367	47.97
	3-4	207	27.06
	1 -2	93	12.16
	N = 765		

Average Hours = 5 (4.79) hrs.

TIME DEVOTED TO LECTURE/DISCUSSION/PRACTICAL

As regards the time devoted to lecture by resource persons, discussions and practical by participants, from the results given in Table - 5.16 it is seen that resource persons devote more time to delivering lectures. For computing average time, the midpoints of each class interval (Table - 5.16) were multiplied by respective frequency and then the summation of the products was divided by total number of respondents. It should be noted that frequency of 'No Response' has been excluded from the respective numbers.

However, a detail analysis in Table - 5.16 presents that all the responses were classified into six groups including 'No Response' category. From the results it is clear that participants desire one and half hours (1.35 hrs.) on an average to be devoted to lecture by resource persons. Similarly, (a) 2.48% participants are of the view that 4 to5 hours should be devoted to the same; (b) 3 to 4 hrs. in case of 4.31%; (c) 2 to 3 hrs. in case of 16.73%; (d) 1 to 2 hrs. in case of 26.01%; and minimum up to one hour in case of 46.93%, respectively. But 3.53% participants remain silent in this regard.

Moreover, participants with regard to discussions state that least time, i.e. 0.91 hrs. on an average, should be devoted to the same. Again, they observe that the time devoted to discussion should be; (a) maximum 3 to 4 hrs. (0.26%); (b) 2 to 3 hrs. (4.44%); (c) 1 to 2 hrs. (29.02%); and (d) minimum up to one hr. (61.7%), respectively. Only 4.58% participants are having no response in this regard.

Similarly, the results also show that participants like about one hour (0.93 hrs.) on an average to be given to practical. They also opine that time devoted to the same should be (according to the frequency of mentioning) 1.7%, 4.84%, 26.27%, and 62.75% of 3 to 4 hours, 2 to 3 hours, 1 to 2 hours and minimum up to one hour/ respectively. Again 4.44% participants have kept themselves away from responding to the same.

Table- 5.16: Time Devoted to Lecture by Resource Persons, Discussions and Practical

PFQ: How much time should be devoted daily to lecture by resource persons, discussions and practicals by participants?	Time in hrs.	Lecture f	Lecture %	Discussion f	Discussion %	Practical f	Practical %
	4-5	19	2.48	-	-	-	-
	3-4	33	4.31	02	0.26	13	1.70
	2-3	128	16.73	34	4.44	37	4.84
	1-2	199	26.01	222	29.02	201	26.27
	0-1	359	46.93	472	61.7	480	62.75
	No Response	27	3.53	35	4.58	34	4.44
		N = 738		N = 730		N = 731	

Average Time = 1.35 hrs. 0.91 hrs 0.93 hrs. N = 765, but for computing 'Average Time' the frequency of 'No Response' has been excluded from the respective No.

TIME DEVOTED TO COURSE COMPONENTS OF THE ASCs

With regard to the suitability of time devoted to course components of the OPs, the responses of the participants have been analyzed and presented in Table - 5.17. The range shown in this Table implies the minimum and maximum time (in hours), which was devoted to each course component during the OPs. Similarly, average time mentioned in the Table have been found by multiplying the time (in hours) with the frequency of mentioning, respectively and then the resulting time scores were summed up and was divided by total number of respondents.

According to the opinion of the participants, (a) as high as 8 hours (7.89 hrs.) on an average, ranging from 1 hr. to 90 hrs. was devoted to the Component 'A' (Linkages between Society, Environment, Development and Education); (b) ranging from 1 hr. to 66 hrs. it was about 7 hours (6.97 hrs) on an average, to Component 'B' (Philosophy of Education, Indian System of Education and Pedagogy); (c) the least time was devoted to Component 'C (Subject Up gradation); i.e. about 6 hrs. (5.7 hrs.) ranging from 1 hrs to 60 hrs. and (d) about six and half hours (6.5 hrs), ranging from 1 hr. to 72 hrs. was devoted to component 'D' (Management and Personality Development) on an average, respectively.

Table - 5.17: Time Devoted to Four Components of the Course

PFQ: How much time, in your opinion, devoted to:	Range	Ave. Time
(a) Component 'A' (Linkages between Society, Environment,and Education)	1 - 90 hrs.	7.89 hrs
(b) Component 'B' (Philosophy of Education, Indian System of Education and Pedagogy)	1 - 66 hrs.	6.97 hrs.
(c) Component 'C (Subject Up gradation)	1 - 60 hrs.	5.7 hrs.
(d) Component 'D' (Management and Personality Development)	1 - 72 hrs.	6.5. hrs.

N = 765

SUITABILITY OF TIME PROVIDED FOR HOLDING DISCUSSION

The suitability of the duration of the OPs in terms of time devoted to holding discussion with resource persons has been found out through the perception of the participating teachers of the OPs. The results, in details, are presented in Table -5.18.

The responses of the participants to a question pertaining to suitability of the time spent for holding discussion with resource persons during the course indicate that a good majority of them, i.e. 68.37% observe that the time provided is quite sufficient and the same is not sufficient for 29 41%; and only 2.22% remain silent on this issue.

Table- 5.18: Suitability of Time Provided for Holding Discussion with Resource Persons

PFQ: Is sufficient time provided for holding discussion with the resource persons during the course?		f	%
	Yes	523	68.37
	No	225	29.41
	No Response	17	2.22

N = 765

WORTHWHILENESS OF THE TIME AND MONEY OF THE OPS.

As regards the worthwhileness of the time and money spent for organizing the OPs, the participants were asked a question to respond. The responses analysed and presented in Table — 5.19 reveal that most of the participants (71.50%) perceive the OPs worth the time and money spent to attend them, and the same is not worthwhile for only 22.35%., while 6.15% do not give their comment, on the issue.

Table - 5.19: Worthwhileness of the Time and Money Spent in the OPs

PFQ: Are the Orientation Programmes worth the time, and money spent to attend them?		f	%
	Yes	547	71.50
	No	171	22.35
	No Response	47	6.15

N = 765

SUGGESTIONS

The participants of the OPs were asked to give some suggestions to improve the suitability of the duration and organisation of the programmes. They have enlisted many suggestions in this regard. But, eliminating the overlapping and irrelevant points a list was prepared to suggest for further improvement of the organisation and duration of the course. The most frequently mentioned of them are:

1. OP should be organized during holidays.
2. It should be organized for the newly entrants in the teaching profession (1st year in the profession) only.
3. Long session of mere delivering lectures should be avoided. More time should be provided to practical and laboratory work, computer and Internet, seminar and co-curricular activities.
4. Number of session should be reduced to 4 allotting one hour per session.
5. More time should be given to the participants' involvement. There must be discussion after every lecture, and more time should be allotted for general discussion/interaction with resource persons than delivering lectures.
6. Participants should be invited from outside university and state for all disciplines.

7. There should be one proforma (standard) to organize the orientation programme for all ASCs in the country/ India.

8. Short break should be given in between two sessions.

CHAPTER-VI

CO-CURRICULAR AND FINANCIAL SYSTEM

In this Chapter, first the systems adopted for providing co-curricular activities, both on the campus and off the campus, to the participants undergoing OPs in the ASCs, India have been studied and analysed. Thereafter, an attempt has been made to evaluate their effectiveness to provide feedback to the teachers. Finally, this chapter evaluates the financial facilities provided to the teachers in terms of the feedback collected from them.

CO-CURRICULAR ACTIVITIES

As regards co-curricular activities of the OPs, the participants' opinion about the necessity of such activities was sought. The responses given by the participants in Table -6.1 show that most of the participants, i.e. 82.22% feel that some co-curricular activities are essential in the orientation programmes. However, only 15.69% are of the opinion that such activities are not essential while 2.09% participants could not respond to the question.

Table -6.1: Co-curricular Activities

PFQ: Do you think that some co-curricular activities are essential in the orientation programme?		f	%
	Yes	629	82.22
	No	120	15.69
	No Response	16	2.09

N = 765

Moreover, the next question asked to the participants was to know as to if some co-curricular activities were essential in the OP. The responses collected from the participants in this regard are mentioned below:

ACTIVITIES IN THE INSTITUTION (ON THE CAMPUS)

Co-curricular activities which the participants felt essential are; (a) cultural programmes including educational drama, dance, music, etc. (b) literary programmes like debate, quiz, recitation, creative writing, etc. (c) some indoor games; (d) psychological and educational games; (e) role playing in educational films; (f) exhibition of modern scientific and technological aids; (g) preparation of magazine, bulletin board etc; (h) physical education and training; and (i) preparation of some models related to the subject.

ACTIVITIES OUTSIDE THE INSTITUTION (OFF THE CAMPUS)

The participants also felt essential of co-curricular activities frequently mentioned in the category of activities outside the institution are; (a) visit to library, educational institutions, science and technological institutions, historical places, research institutions, NGOs etc; (b) community visit and environmental awareness programmes; (c) NSS programmes; (d) outdoor games; and (e) literary campaign in remote areas.

SATISFACTION WITH CO-CURRICULAR ACTIVITIES

The responses of the participants to question as to whether or not they are satisfied with co-curricular activities offered by the ASCs reveal that the highest 48.76% (Table - 6.2) participants are satisfied with the co-curricular activities offered in the orientation programme; but as many as 43.53% participants are not satisfied with the same, whereas 7.71% of them could not respond to the question.

Table - 6.2: Satisfaction with Co-curricular Activities

PFQ: Are you satisfied with the co-curricular activities offered in the orientation programme?		f	%
	Yes	373	48.76
	No	333	43.53
	No Response	59	7.71

N = 765

It is evident that co-curricular activities offered in the OPs are not satisfactory as perceived by 43.53% participants (Table - 6.2). Hence, such activities need to be improved in subsequent programmes. With this intention in mind participants were asked to give some suggestions for the improvement of co-curricular activities in the OPs. The most relevant suggestions provided by the participants are given below:

(i) Separate fund for co-curricular activities should be maintained.

(ii) Facilities for playing and exhibiting co-curricular activities should be available in the ASC.

(iii) Co-curricular programmes should be pre-planned well before the commencement of the programme.

FINANCIAL SYSTEM

In respect the financial system of the OPs, the responses collected from the participants reveal that; (a) in case of 63.53% participants, T.A and DA. given are satisfactory; whereas 34.63% participants are not satisfied with T.A. and D.A. given in the OP and 1.83% could not respond; (b) only 35.16% participants are satisfied with hostel facilities provided to them and majority of them, i.e. 52.68% are not satisfied, whereas 12.16% could not give their opinion to the question asked; (c) books and other reading materials provided are found satisfactory by 44.9% participants, but majority of them 52.55% are not satisfied and 2.48%

Table - 6.3: Financial System of Orientation Programnmes

PFQ: Are you satisfied with:	Yes		No		No Response	
	f	%	f	%	f	%
(a) T. A. and DA. given	486	63.53	265	34.64	14	1.83
(b) Hostel facilities provided	269	35.16	403	52.68	93	12.16
(c) Books and other reading materials provided	344	44.97	402	52.55	19	2.48
(d) Library facilities	418	54.64	332	43.40	15	1.96
(e) The access of the books, journals of the study centre	341	44.58	394	51.50	30	3.92
(f) Facilities provided to you for field visits	330	43.14	400	52.29	35	4.58
(g) Physical conditions of the ASC	431	56.34	278	36.34	56	7.32
PFQ: On the whole, are you satisfied with the financial aspects of the OPs?	459	60.00	246	32.16	60	7.84

N=765

participants could not respond; (d) most of the participants, i.e. 54.64% are satisfied with library facilities but 43.40% find the same unsatisfactory, whereas 1 96% remained neutral in this regard; (e) only 44.58% participants are satisfied with the access to the books, journals etc. at the study centre, but majority of the participants (51.50%) are not satisfied and 3.92% participants could not respond; (f) similarly, only 43.14% participants are satisfied with facilities provided for field visits, but majority of them i.e. 52.29% find the same unsatisfactory, whereas 4.58% were having no opinion on the same; and (g) majority of participants (56.34%) observe that they are satisfied with physical conditions of the ASC, but the same was not satisfactory to 36.34% participants, whereas 7.32% could not respond to the issue.

Moreover, the participants were also asked a question; "On the whole, are you satisfied with the financial aspect of the OP?" The results presented in the same Table - 6.3 reveal that 60% respondents are satisfied with the financial aspects of the OPs and 32.16% find the same unsatisfactory whereas, 7.84% kept themselves away to comment upon the same.

CHAPTER-VII

RESOURCE PERSONS

The success of the OPs offered by the ASCs in India, no doubt, to a large extent depends on the quality of the instructors available and are engaged. What criteria do the institutions for their selection generally adopt? Who identifies the resource persons? Are they suitable in terms of knowledge, presentation and as a teacher? Whether or not the participants are satisfied with their RPs in terms of their background relevant to the content of the course? These are some of the questions addressed to in this chapter.

SELECTION CRITERIA OF RESOURCE PERSONS (RPs)

With an intention to find out the selection criteria of RPs for the OPs, the Directors and staff of the ASCs were provided with a list of six criteria relating to the selection of the RPs under the question (SOPQ) number 1 as given in the Table 7.1. They were asked to put a tick mark (√) if given criterion was applicable in their case. The results of this study indicate that 70.83% RPs are selected on the basis of their scholarship; in case of 54.17% RPs, their successful teachership is the criteria of their selection; while 79.17% i.e. a large number of respondents state that selection criteria of RPs for the OPs is both scholarship and teachership. Similarly, 79.17% staffs take into account the subject/area specialization of the RPs, but most of the ASCs/respondents (91.67%) feel participants' feedbacks as the important criteria of selection of RPs for the ASCs. Again,70.83% respondents also take into account the course coordinator's suggestions while selecting resource persons of the OPs.

Table- 7.1: Selection Criteria of Resource Persons

SOPQ 1: While selecting resource persons, what criteria is generally taken into account by your institution? Please mark (√)	f	%
(a) Scholarship	17	70.83
(b) Successful teachership	13	54.17
(c) Both scholarship and teachership	19	79.17
(d) Subject/area specialization	19	79.17
(e) Participants' feedbacks	22	91.67
(f) Course co-ordinator's suggestions	17	70.83

N =24, but multiple responses possible

INTERNAL/EXTERNAL RESOURCE PERSONS

With regard to the invitation of the resource persons for the OPs, the staffs of the ASCs were asked a question (SOPQ2) for which three possible responses were given. The results presented in the Table 7.2 show that only 12.5% RPs invited to the ASCs are external; similarly, 29.17% internal and local RPs are invited to the ASCs. It is important to note that majority of the resource persons, i.e. 58.33% invited to the ASCs are both external and internal.

Table - 7.2: External/Internal RPs

SOPQ 2: Resource persons invited to the ASC are mainly: (Please mark V)	f	%
(a) External Resource Persons.	03	12.50
(b) Internal and Local Resource Persons.	07	29.17
(c) Both External and internal	14	58.33

N = 24

CO-OPERATION FROM RESOURCE PERSONS

The staffs of the ASCs were asked whether they get full co-operation from the RPs in time. The results in the Table 7.3 show an encouraging observation that the ASCs get full co-operation, i.e. cent percent (100%) from the RPs in time when needed.

Table - 7.3: Co-operation From Resource Persons

SOPQ 3: Do you get full co-operation from resource persons in time?		f	%
	Yes	24	100
	No	00	N.A.

N = 24

IDENTIFICATION OF RPs

An enquiry into the identification of RPs for the OPs; indicates that in 66.67% cases, both Director and Course Co-ordinators identify resource persons. However, the Director identifies 37.15% resource persons, whereas in 25% cases, Course Coordinators alone do identification of RPs. Similarly, in 8.83% cases, Advisory Committee of the ASC also is involved in identifying RPs for the OPs. Thus, it reflects that identification of RPs for the OPs is a joint business/ concerns of Directors, Course Co-ordinators and Advisory Committee of the ASCs. Further, it is clear that for the identification of the RPs, few ASCs take help from references of sister ASCs and also take into account the suggestions made by the PG Departmental Committee of the concerned university.

Table - 7.4: Identification of Resource Persons

SOPQ 4: Identification of RPs is mainly done by:	f	%
(a) The Director	09	37.15
(b) The Course Co-ordinators	06	25.00
(c) Both Director and Course Coordinators	16	66.67
(d) Advisory Committee of the ASC	02	08.83

N = 24, but multiple responses possible

SUITABILITY OF THE RPs

The results in Table 7.1 reveal that several criteria such as scholarship, successful teachership, combination of scholarship and teachership, subject/area specialization, participants' feedbacks, suggestions of course coordinators, etc. are taken into account by most of the ASCs while selecting RPs for the OPs. But, how suitable the RPs selected are on the basis of these criteria for teaching different course components of the OPs calls for a significant study. Moreover, as the RPs are invited for the benefit of the teacher participants their opinions as to what they think about the suitability of the RPs and their background relevant to the course content is of extreme importance. Thus, in this section, an attempt has been made to evaluate the RPs and their background relevant to the course content of the OPs in the light of the feedback received from the participants.

SUITABILITY OF THE RPs IN TERMS OF THE COURSE CONTENT

The participants included in the sample were asked a question as to if they are satisfied with the RPs invited to deliver each course component of the OPs.

The results in table 7.5 reveal that 72.16% participants are satisfied with the RPs in regard to the Component 'A' (Linkages between Society, Environment, Development and Education) and 20.92% are not satisfied with RPs invited for the Component 'A'; whereas, 6.93% participants do not comment. With regard to the Component 'B' (Philosophy of Education, Indian Education System and Pedagogy), majority of the participants, i.e. 63.66% perceive that RPs invited for this component are satisfactory; whereas 27.84% participants are not satisfied with the RPs; and 8.50% are silent on this issue. Similarly, 54.25% participants are of the opinion that RPs invited for the Component 'C (Subject Upgradation) are satisfactory; whereas in case of 35.69% participants, RPs are not satisfactory; and 10.07% do not respond to this question. Again, 59.87% participants are satisfied with the RPs invited for the Component 'D' (Management and Personality Development); 29.80% are not satisfied with the same while 10.33% are having no response to the question. Moreover, an overview of the results indicates that 62.48% participants are satisfied with the RPs invited for course components of the OPs; 28.56% participants are not satisfied with the RPs; and 8.95% are having no response to the question. Thus, it reflects that in case of 37.52% participants, the RPs are not satisfactory in terms of the course components of the OPs. The questions: Who are these RPs, What are the motivation and aspiration level of those 37.52% participants? etc. call for a further empirical study.

Table - 7.5: Suitability of the RPs in Terms of Course Components

PFQ 1: Are you satisfied with the RPs invited for each Course Component of the OP?	Yes		No		No Response	
	f	%	f	%	f	%
(a) Component 'A'	552	72.16	160	20.92	53	6.93
(b) Component B'	487	63.66	213	27.84	65	8.50
(c) Component 'C'	415	54.25	273	35.69	77	10.07
(d) Component 'D'	458	59.87	228	29.80	79	10.33
Total (N = 765 X 4 = 3060)	1912	62.48	874	28.56	274	8.95

SUITABILITY OF THE RPs IN TERMS OF KNOWLEDGE IN THE SUBJECT, PRESENTATION, INTERACTION AND AS A TEACHER

In order to evaluate the suitability of the RPs in terms of their knowledge in the subject, presentation, interaction and as a teacher, the participants were asked to rate these aspects in terms of a four points scale, i.e. moderate, good, very good and excellent.

The overall results in Table 7.6 reveal that on the whole, the highest number of participants, i.e. 42.68% perceive the RPs good in terms of their knowledge in the subject, presentation, interaction and as a teacher. In other words, 42.22, 43.79, 40.52 and 44.18 percent participants perceive their RPs good in terms of knowledge in the subject, presentation, interaction, and as a teacher, respectively.

It seems that all these four desirable qualities within the RPs are, on the average, perceived very good by almost every fourth

Table-7.6: Suitability of the RPs in Terms of Knowledge in the Subject, Presentation, Interaction and As a Teacher

PFQ: Below are mentioned the suitability of the resource persons in terms of their knowledge in the subject, presentation, interaction and as a teacher. You are requested to rate by putting (√) against each aspect of the RPs in terms of their suitability on a four points scale.

Aspects	Moderate		Good		Very Good		Excellent		No Response	
	f	%	f	%	f	%	f	%	f	%
(a) Knowledge in the subject	86	11.24	323	42.22	202	26.41	126	16.47	28	3.66
(b) Presentation	137	17.91	395	43.79	202	26.41	60	7.84	31	4.05
(c) Interaction	180	23.53	310	40.52	178	23.27	74	9.67	23	3.01
(d) As a Teacher	94	12.29	338	44.18	187	24.44	112	14.64	44	4.44
Total (N=765x4=3060)	497	16.24	1306	42.68	769	25.13	372	12.16	116	3.79

participants, i.e. 25.13% (approximately 25%); whereas these are perceived excellent by almost every eighth, i.e. 12.16% participants (approximately 12.50%). However, observing each aspect separately, it is found that: (a) in case of 26.41% and 16.47% RPs have very good and excellent knowledge in the subject, respectively, (b) in 26.41% cases presentation of the RPs is very good which is excellent only in 7.84% cases; (c) in 23.27% cases, very good interaction was there between RPs and participants, which is excellent only in 9.67% cases; and (d) 24.44% participants perceive RP as very good teacher, whereas 14.64% perceive them as excellent.

However, it is worth mentioning that on the whole 16.24% participants perceive RPs to be moderate in terms of: (a) knowledge in the subject (11.24%); (b) presentation (17.91%); (c) interaction (23.53%); and (d) as a teacher (12.29%). But 3.79% participants on the average, are reluctant to respond to the question.

SATISFACTION WITH RPs

In an attempt to ascertain if the participants are satisfied with their RPs, the results in Table 7.7 show that on the whole, 75.95% participants are satisfied with RPs and their background relevant to the course content of the OPs, whereas 21.96% are dissatisfied and only 2.09% respondents do not give their opinion in this regard.

Table - 7.7: Satisfaction with the RPs

PFQ On the whole, are you satisfied with your resource persons and their background relevant to the content of the course?		f	%
	Yes	581	75.95
	No	168	21.96
	No Response	16	2.09

N = 765

Moreover, the next question in the questionnaire invited suggestions from those participants who are not satisfied (21.96% in Table 7.7) with RPs and their background relevant to the course content of the OPs. A few relevant and most important suggestions given by the participants are:

(i) Competent and devoted teachers/experts of the specialized field with sound research as well as teaching experience should be invited as RPs.

(ii) National level renowned persons from other universities should be invited as resource persons.

(iii) The U.G.C. with the help of National Assessment and Accreditation Council (NAAC), should prepare and publish a list of RPs for invitation to ASCs.

(iv) RPs should be selected on the basis of participants' feedback.

(v) Retired persons should not be invited as RPs.

(vi) RPs in the area of Communication and Information Technology should be invited.

CHAPTER-VIII

Methodology Followed in Orientation Programme

In this Chapter the existing system pertaining to methods and aids adopted, and interactions offered to the participants undergoing OPs in the ASCs in India have been surveyed. Specifically an attempt has been made to evaluate the entire system of methodology followed for delivering course contents in the light of the perceptions of the staffs and feedback from the participants of the ASCs in India.

METHODS ADOPTED

In order to ascertain the methods adopted for delivering course content in the OPs, the Directors and staff of the ASCs were asked to respond a question as to "what methods are adopted for delivering course content in orientation programmes?" There were twelve possible methods mentioned in the questionnaire to respond.

The results given in Table 8.1 indicate that as many as 87.5% ASCs in India use (a) lecture-cum group discussion, and (b) lecture-cum discussion-cum seminar methods for delivering course content to the participants. Similarly, every second ASCs (50%) adopt (i) lecture-cum group discussion-cum seminar, and (ii) symposia/ workshop methods for delivering course content in the OPs. However, every two of the three ASCs (66.67%) use(a) lecture-cum demonstration, and (b) brainstorming methods. It is worth noting that in between 66.67% and 87.17% cases, the ASCs adopt four different methods for delivering course content in the OPs. These are arranged below according to their frequency of occurrence:

(a) books review and paper presentation (79.17%); (b) field visits/ studies/surveys (79.17%); (c) assignments (70.83%) and (d) microteaching session (70.83%). Further, it is found that every third ASCs (33.33%) use self-study method in the OPs; whereas role play/games is used only by 29.17% of the ASCs for delivering course content to their participants.

Table - 8.1: Methods Adopted for Delivering Course Content

SOPQ: What methods are adopted for delivering course content in Orientation Programmes?	f	%
(a) Lecture-cum group discussion.	21	87.50
(b) Lecture-cum group discussion-cum seminar	12	50
(c) Lecture-cum demonstration.	16	66.67
(d) Lecture-cum discussion-cum seminar.	21	87.50
(e) Assignments.	17	70.83
(f) Book reviews and paper presentation.	19	79.17
(g) Role play/games.	07	29.17
(h) Brain storming.	16	66.67
(i) Field visits/studies/surveys.	19	79.17
(j) Symposia/workshop.	12	50
(k) Microteaching.	17	70.83
(1) Self study.	08	33.33

N = 24, but multiple responses possible

SELECTION OF METHODS

As regards the selection of methodologies, the staff of the ASCs were asked a question; "who selects the methodologies for various course components?" There were three possible responses.

The results presented in Table 8.2 reveal that in case of every 8th ASCs, i.e. 12.50%, the staffs of the institution select the methodologies for various course components; whereas in case of every sixth ASCs (16.67%), the methodologies for various course components are selected by the resource persons. It is encouraging to note that in most of the cases (70.83%), both the staff of the ASCs and the resource persons get involved in selecting the methodologies for various course components of the OPs.

Table - 8.2: Selection of Methodologies for various Course Components

SOPQ: Who selects the methodologies for various course components?	f	%
(a) The staff of the institution.	03	12.50
(b) The resource persons	04	16.67
(c) Both the staff and the resource persons	17	70.83

N = 24

COMPULSORY METHODOLOGIES ADOPTED IN THE OPs

An inquiry into the compulsory methodologies adopted by the ASCs for delivering the course content in the OPs, reveals that (Table 8.3) assignment is the compulsory method of every two of the three ASCs (66.67%); in almost all ASCs (95.83%), paper presentation is compulsory, in 54.17% ASCs, book review is used as compulsory method; and microteaching session is compulsory in 45.83% ASCs. Besides these, the respondents observe that warming up session including group song, silent sitting, report writing, etc. are some of the compulsory methods used by few ASCs for delivering course content in the OPs.

Moreover, the staffs were also asked to give a rank (1,2,3,4 etc.) to each of the four methods used as compulsory (Table 8.3) according to the emphasis given. Rank 1 indicates foremost used and rank 4 indicates least used. A score of 4 was given to rank 1, and a score of 1 was given to rank 4. Similarly, rank 2 and rank 3 were scored as 3 and 2, respectively. The frequency of each rank was multiplied by the respective rank score and summation of these scores provided the total rank scores for each method adopted. Accordingly, ranks were found on the basis of rank scores.

From the results, it is observed that the ASCs give the highest importance to paper presentation (rank 1. with rank score 42), and the least importance on book review (rank 4, with rank score 29). Similarly, the ASCs in India give second and third ranks to the assignments and microteaching methods, respectively.

Table - 8.3: Compulsory Methodologies Adopted for Delivering Course Content

SOPQ: Which one of the following is compulsory at your institution?	f	%	Rank	Rank Score
(a) Assignments	16	66.67	2	31
(b) Paper presentation	23	95.83	1	42
(c) Books review	13	54.17	4	29
(d) Micro teaching session	11	45.83	3	30

N = 24, but multiple responses possible

SUITABILITY OF THE METHODOLOGY ADOPTED

In order to evaluate the suitability of the methodology adopted in the OPs, the participating teachers were provided with a list of twelve (12) methods possibly adopted in the OPs and were asked to mark the methods which were adopted, and to rank each method to the extent it was adopted.

The results shown in Table 8.4 show the ranks according to the rank scores of each method adopted in the OPs. The rank scores were found out by applying the methods given in Table 8.3. The results in this study indicate that participants of the OPs have assigned rank 1 (with rank score 7197) to the lecture-cum group discussion as the maximum adopted method in the OPs and self study as the least adopted method with rank 12 (rank score 2853). In between these two methods, other methods adopted in the OPs as perceived by the participants in order of ratings are lecture-cum demonstration (rank 2); lecture-cum discussion-cum seminar (rank 3); lecture-cum group discussion-cum simulation (rank 4); assignments (rank 5); books review and paper presentation (rank 6); field visits/studies/surveys (rank 7), microteaching session (rank 8); symposia/workshop (rank 9); brainstorming (rank 10); and role play/ games (rank 11).

Table - 8.4: Suitability of the Methods Adopted for Delivering Course Content

PFQ:Which of the following methods are adopted for delivering course content in the OP (Please give tick mark if adopted and rank 1,2,3... etc. using Rank 1 for the method maximum adopted and use. 2,3,4.. etc. for other lesser-adopted methods).	f	rank	rank score
(a) Lecture-cum group discussion	690	1	7197
(b) Lecture-cum group discussion-cum simulation.	486	4	4710
(c) Lecture-cum demonstration	595	2	5887
(d) Lecture-cum discussion-cum seminar	559	3	5381
(e) Assignments	496	5	4336
(f) Book reviews and paper presentation	494	6	4267
(g) Role play/games	382	11	3213
(h) Brainstorming	405	10	3217
(i) Field visits/studies/surveys	483	7	3965
(j) Symposia/workshop	397	9	3237
(k) Microteaching session	427	8	3428
(1) Self study	357	12	2853

N = 765, but multiple responses possible.

SATISFACTION WITH THE METHODOLOGY ADOPTED

The participants of the OPs were asked a question "Are you satisfied with the methods adopted for the presentation of the course?" The results given in Table 8.5 reveal that most of the participants, i.e. 69.15% are satisfied with the methods adopted for the presentation of the course content in the OPs. It is also seen that every fourth participants, i.e. 26.14% are not satisfied with the methodology adopted for the presentation of the course content in the OPs, while 4.71% participants do not give their opinion on the issue.

Table - 8.5: Satisfaction with Methods adopted for the Presentation of Course Content

PFQ: Are you satisfied with the methods adopted for the presentation of the course content?		f	%
	Yes	529	69.15
	No	200	26.14
	No Response	36	4.71

N=765

Moreover, for further discussion the Table 8.5 requires an in depth study of the causes for the dissatisfaction of the participants (26.14% in Table 8.5) with the methodology adopted and the suggestions for the improvement of the methods to be adopted for the presentation of the course content in the OPs. In this regard, the next question of the questionnaire invited suggestions from those participants who were not satisfied with the methods adopted for the presentation of the course content in the OPs. Participants have extended many suggestions for improving the methodology. Eliminating the overlapping and irrelevant, some of the constructive suggestions frequently mentioned are listed below:

(i) Every lecture should be followed by group discussion.

(ii) More visual demonstration is needed.

(iii) Field visits/studies/surveys should be conducted frequently.

(iv) Lecture-cum demonstration-cum seminar should be conducted.

(v) Microteaching should be made compulsory for each participant.

(vi) Workshop/symposia should be conducted.

(vii) Assignments should be introduced.

(viii) Role play/games should be emphasized.

(ix) Some experimental methods should be introduced.

MEDIA AND AIDS

In order to ascertain the teaching media and aids adopted for delivering course content in the OPs, the Directors and staff of the ASCs were asked a question to respond which had five possible responses. They were also asked to give a rank to the extent each media and aids was adopted by their institutions.

The results given in Table 8.6 reveal that (a) almost all the ASCs (95.83%) adopt overhead projector in delivering course content in the OPs; (b) slide projector is used by 87.50%; (c) 79.17% ASCs adopt TV and VCR; and also computer; and (d) 70.83% ASCs adopt educational films while delivering course content in the OPs in India.

However, ASCs assign Rank 1 to the adoption of overhead projector with 40 rank score; rank 2 to the use of slide projector; rank 3 to the use of TV and VCR; rank 4 to computer and rank 5 with rank score 14 to the use of educational films in delivering course content in the OPs. Again, the results indicate that though equal numbers of ASCs (79.17%) adopt both TV and VCR, and Computer in the OPs, but the former one (TV and VCR) was more emphasized (Rank 3) than the later (computer Rank 4).

Table - 8.6: Teaching Media and Aids Adopted in Delivering Course Content

SOPQ: What media and aids, in your opinion, are adopted in delivering course content in OPs? (Please give ranks 1,2,3 etc. to the extent media and aids are adopted).	f	%	Rank	Rank Score
(a) Overhead Projector	23	95.83	01	40
(b) TV and VCR	19	79.17	03	23
(c) Slide Projector.	21	87.50	02	26
(d) Computer.	19	79.17	04	18
(e) Educational Films	17	70.83	05	14

N = 24, but multiple responses possible.

SELECTION OF TEACHING MEDIA AND AIDS

With regard to the selection of teaching media and aids, the results indicate that in case of every fifth ASCs (20.83%), the course co-ordinators of the ASCs select the teaching media and aids for various course components offered in the OPs; in 45.83% cases, teaching media and aids are selected by the resource persons. It is interesting to note that both the course coordinators and the resource persons select the teaching media and aids for various course components in every two of the three ASCs, i.e. 66.67%. However, only in 4.17% cases, other institutions prepare the teaching media and aids used for various course components for the OPs of the ASCs.

Table-8.7: Selection of the Teaching Media and Aids for Various Course Components

SOPQ: Who selects the teaching media and aids for various course components offered in your institution?	f	%
(a) The course coordinators of the ASC.	05	20.83
(b) The resource persons.	11	45.83
(c) Both the course coordinators and resource persons.	16	66.67
(d) Use of media and aids prepared by other institutions.	01	4.17

N = 24, but multiple responses possible

SUITABILITY OF THE MEDIA AND AIDS

In order to find out the suitability of the media and aids used for delivering course content in the OPs of the ASCs in India, participants of the programmes were asked a question to respond which provided with five possible responses in addition to an open-ended response to list any other media and aids were used besides those mentioned in the questionnaire. They were also asked to give rank to each media and aids to the extent they were used in delivering the course content of the programme. Accordingly, ranks and the corresponding rank scores of each media and aids used were found out by applying the method given in Table 8.8.

The results shown in Table 8.8 show that overhead projector is the maximum used media in delivering the course content in the OPs, which has been ranked 1 (with rank score 2468) by the participants; slide projector receives rank 2; TV. and V.C.R. rank 3; computer rank 4; and educational films is least used media and aids in delivering course content of the OPs which has been ranked 5 by the participants of the programme. Further, the participants reveal that some other media and aids such as *black-board,* charts, *maps, paper cutting,* manuscripts, *laboratory instruments,* floppy discs, etc. were also used in delivering course content of the OPs.

Table - 8.8: Media and Aids used for Delivering Course Content

PFQ: Which of the following media and aids are adopted for delivering course content in the OPs (Please give tick mark if adopted and rank 1,2,3,....etc. using rank 1 for the media/aids maximum adopted and use 2,3,4,...etc. for other lesser adopted media/aids)	f	Rank	Rank Score
(a) Overhead Projector.	641	1	2468
(b) T.V. and V.C.R.	427	3	1401
(c) Slide Projector	550	2	1893
(d) Computer	389	4	1113
(e) Educational Films	97	5	255

N = 765, but multiple responses possible

SATISFACTION WITH THE MEDIA/AIDS ADOPTED

The participants of the OPs were asked to respond to a question: "Are you satisfied with the media/aids adopted for the presentation of the course content?" The results presented in Table 8.9 reveal that most of the participants (62.48%) are satisfied with the media/aids adopted for the presentation of the course content in the OPs. However, every third participant (33 99%) are not satisfied with the media/aids adopted for the presentation of the course content in the programme, while 3.53% of the participants do not respond to the question.

Table - 8.9: Satisfaction with the Media/Aids Adopted for the Presentation of the Course

PFQ: Are you satisfied with the media/aids adopted for the presentation of the course content?		f	%
	Yes	478	62.48
	No	260	33.99
	No Response	27	3.53

N = 765

Moreover, participants who are not satisfied with the media/ aids adopted in the OPs(33.99% in Table 8.9) were asked an open-ended question to suggest for further improvement of the media/ aids to be used in the OPs. The suggestions in this regard are as follows:

(a) Computer/internet should be used.

(b) Educational films/documents prepared by UGC should be shown.

(c) The frequency of using T.V. and V.C.R. should be increased.

(d) All modern media should be utilized.

(e) Projector should be used.

(f) Participants should be asked to develop teaching aids/ models.

MODE OF INTERACTIONS OFFERED

With regard to the mode of interaction, the staffs of the ASCs were asked a question as to "What is the mode of interaction between the participants and the resource persons?" There were five possible responses.

The results given in Table 8.10 show that the mode of interaction is exchange of views/ideas between the participants and resource persons in most of the ASCs, i.e. 83.33%. Similarly, in 83.33% ASCs also, paper presentation/ seminar is the mode of interaction between the participants and resource persons. Moreover, group discussion is the mode of interaction in 79.17% ASCs. However, compulsory question answer session is the mode of interaction between participants and resource persons in every third (33.33%) ASCs; whereas, in case of every fourth (25.00%) ASCs, book review are the mode of interaction between the participants and resource persons in the OPs of the ASCs.

Table- 8.10: Mode of Interaction Between Participants and Experts

SOPQ: What is the mode of interaction between the participants and the resource persons?		
(a) Exchange of views/ideas between the participants and resource persons.	20	83.33
(b) Compulsory question answer session.	08	33.33
(c) Group discussion.	19	79.17
(d) Paper presentation/seminar	20	83.33
(e) Book review	06	25.00

N = 24, but multiple responses possible

INITIATION OF INTERACTION

The staffs of the ASCs were asked a question to respond as to "who initiates the interaction?" The results of this study in Table 8.11 indicate that in most of the cases (70.83%), the resource persons initiate the interaction between participants and resource persons; in every two of the three ASCs (66.67%), interaction is initiated by the participants; in every second ASCs (50%), both the staff and the resource persons initiate the interaction, and in every third (33.33%) ASCs, the interactions are initiated by the staff of the institution.

Table - 8.11: Initiation of Interaction

SOPQ: Who initiates the interaction?	f	%
(a) The staff of the institution.	08	33.33
(b) The resource persons.	17	70.83
(c) Both the staff and the resource persons.	12	50
(d) The participants.	16	66.67

N = 24, but multiple responses possible.

SUITABILITY OF THE INTERACTION OFFERED TO PARTICIPANTS

In order to find out the suitability of the interaction to participants offered through the perception of the teacher participants of the OPs, participants were provided with a list of five probable processes of interaction among the participants and resource persons. They were asked to mark (√) against the process of interaction, which was ensured, and to give rank to each process to the extent it was ensured.

The results given in Table 8.12 indicate the ranks according to the rank scores of each process of interaction. The rank scores were found out by applying the methods as given in Table 8.3. The results of this study indicate that participants of the OPs assign rank 1 with rank score 2964 to the process of interaction involving exchange of views/ideas between the participants and the resource persons; group discussion receives rank 2 (rank score 2381); paper presentation/ seminar is ranked 3; compulsory question-answer session is ranked 4; and rank 5 is given to book review by the participants.

It appears that though the process of interaction in the form of exchange of views/ideas between the participants and resource persons; and paper presentation/seminar are offered by equal number of the ASCs, i.e. 83.33% in Table 8.10; participants perceive that exchange of ideas/views between the participants and resource persons while undergoing OP is more ensured than paper presentation/seminar. Consequently, they assign rank 1 to the former and rank 3 to the later.

Table- 8.12: The Process of Interaction Among the Participants and Resource Persons

PFQ: Which of the following process of interaction among the participants and resource persons are ensured while undergoing OPs? (Please mark (√) if ensured 1,2,3,4.. etc. using rank 1 for the process of maximum ensured and use 2,3,4,etc. for other lesser ensured interactions).	f	Rank	Rank Score

(a) Exchange of views/ideas between the participants and resource persons	708	1	2964
(b) Compulsory question-answer session.	453	4	1477
(c) Group discussion.	653	2	2381
(d) Paper presentation/seminar	601	3	1916
(e) Book review.	385	5	1052

N = 765, but multiple responses possible

SATISFACTION WITH THE PROCESS OF INTERACTION

The participants were asked a question "Are you satisfied with the process of interaction offered in the OPs?" The results (Table 8.13) reveal that out of 765 participants, 77.12% of them are satisfied with the interaction offered to them during the OPs. However, 19 48% participants are dissatisfied with the same; while 3.4% do not give their comment in regard to the satisfaction they derive from the process of interaction between participants and resource persons in the OPs.

Table - 8.13: Satisfaction with the Process of Interaction Offered

PFQ: Are you satisfied with the process of interactions offered in the OP?		f	%
	Yes	590	77.12
	No	149	19.48
	No Response	26	3.4

N= 765

Moreover, the next question in the questionnaire invited suggestions from those participants who were not satisfied with the process of interaction (19.48% in Table 8.13) offered to them during the OPs. Participants have extended many suggestions for improving the process of interaction between them and resource persons. Eliminating the overlapping and irrelevant, some of the constructive suggestions, frequently mentioned by the participants are listed below:

(a) Every lecture should be followed by interaction for 30 minutes.

(b) More time should be provided for interaction.

(c) There should be lively group-discussion among the participants as well as with the resource persons.

(d) Participation in-group discussion should be compulsory for every teacher.

(e) The frequency of holding seminar/symposia should be increased.

(f) Informal interaction should be encouraged.

(g) Views of the participants should be given weightage.

MODE OF DELIVERY

With an intention to ascertain the mode of delivery of the OPs, the Directors and staff of the ASCs were asked to respond to a question: which of the modes of delivery among methods of presentation, use of media and aids and interaction to participants offered is adopted by the institutions? The results presented in Table 8.14 reveal that in 70.83% ASCs the mode of delivery adopted in the OPs is methods of presentation. Similarly, 70.83% ASCs also use media and aids as the modes of delivery in the OPs; while in (83.33%) cases, the mode of delivery adopted by the ASCs in the OPs is interaction among the participants and between the participants and resource persons invited to deliver course content in the OPs.

Table - 8.14: Mode of Delivery Adopted

SOPQ: Which of the following mode of delivery of the Orientation Programme is adopted in your institution?	f	%
(a) Methods of presentation.	17	70.83
(b) Use of Media and Aids.	17	70.83
(c) Interaction to participants offered	20	83.33

N= 24, but multiple responses possible

PARTICIPANTS' OPINION ON DELIVERING LECTURE AND INDIVIDUAL INTERACTION

In order to study the suitability of the mode of delivery adopted in the OPs of the ASCs, the participants' opinions were invited on a question pertaining to time given for delivering lecture or individual interaction. The results of this study given in Table 8.15 indicate that about two-third, i.e. 66.93% participants are of the opinion that more time should be given to individual interaction during the OPs. However, every fourth participants (25.62%) state that more time should be given to delivering lecture during the OPs; whereas 7.45% participants do not give their opinion on this issue. Thus, this observation support the response of the staff of the ASCs as given in Table 8.14 that the mode of delivery in most of the ASCs (83.33%) is interaction to participants offered.

Table - 8.15: Time Given for Delivering Lecture or Individual Interaction

PFQ: In your opinion, during the OPs should more time be given to delivering lecture or to the individual interaction?		f	%
	Delivering Lecture	196	25.62
	Individual Interaction	512	66.93
	No Response	57	7.45

CHAPTER-IX

THE EVALUATION SYSTEM

The term evaluation, particularly, in the field of education has been used as (a) the determinant of students' level of performance in terms of desired behavioural changes, and (b) the determinant of the effectiveness of the entire educational system. This chapter is concerned with the former type of evaluation i.e., the assessment of participants' performance for the purpose of providing feedback to them. Another important context in which the term evaluation has been used by the ASCs is 'Programme evaluation' i.e., how programmes function, how effective they are and how well are they received by the teacher participants?

In OPs, both formative and summative evaluations are in practice. However, the former assumes a more significant place than the later. The results of the continuous assessment serve, on one hand, the important function of providing timely feedback to the participants to correct themselves, judge for themselves, the value of the efforts they have put in and to monitor their progress accordingly; on the other hand, they have been used to serve as feedback to the course coordinators and resource persons. It is in this background, an attempt has been made to study the practices of assessment adopted by the ASCs in India.

COMPULSORY/VOLUNTARY OR NO EVALUATION

As regards the evaluation of the OPs, the staffs involved in the ASCs were asked a question pertaining to the kind of evaluation (compulsory/voluntary) adopted in the OPs. The responses to the question reveal that two of the every third respondents (66.67% in Table - 9.1) have reported compulsory evaluation used in the OP, while every fourth ASCs (25%) use voluntary evaluation of the course. Moreover, 8.33% respondents have remained silent on the issue.

Table - 9.1: Compulsory, Voluntary or No Evaluation

SOPQ: Do you use any kind of evaluation of the course? (If yes, please give tick mark which applies to your ASC)		f	%
	Compulsory Evaluation	16	66.67
	Voluntary Evaluation	06	25
	No Evaluation	N.A.	N.A.
	No Response	02	8.33

N = 24

KINDS OF EVALUATION

With an intention to find out the kind of evaluation used in the OPs, the staff of the ASCs were asked a question for which three possible responses were provided to respond. The results in Table - 9.2 show that two of the every third respondents (66.67%) observe that the ASCs use self-evaluation by participants in the OPs in terms of their own perceived attitudinal change and skill enhancement; it is programme evaluation by the participants in terms of effectiveness of the programme as reported by 62.50% respondents; and similarly, 50% respondents reveal that the ASCs use formal evaluation of participants in terms of their achievements. Moreover, reporting to an open-ended response, the staffs involved in the ASCs have added some other kinds of evaluation besides those mentioned in the questionnaire such as; (a) informal evaluation including punctuality, conduct and other personal factors of the participants; (b) quiz/tests; and (c) resource persons' evaluation.

Table - 9.2: Kinds of Evaluation Used

SOPQ: Which of the following kinds of evaluation is used by your ASCs?	f	%
(a) Self-evaluation by participants in terms of their own perceived attitudinal change and skill enhancement.	16	66.67
(b) Programme evaluation by the participants in terms of effectivenessof the programme.	15	62.50
(c) Formal evaluation of participants in terms of their achievements.	12	50

N = 24, but multiple responses possible.

EVALUATION OF PERFORMANCE OF THE PARTICIPANTS

As regards evaluation of performance of the participants in the OPs, the staffs involved in the ASCs were asked to respond a question "How performance of participants is evaluated?" They were given a list of four possible responses. The results indicate that three of the every four respondents (75% given in Table - 9.3) have stated that performance of participants in the OPs is evaluated through written assignments for submission; it is written examination as reported by every fourth respondents (25%); 45.83% of them have revealed the same as objective tests; and every eight (12.50%) have reported that performance of the participants in the OP is evaluated through oral tests. Moreover, they have listed some other devices besides those mentioned above for the evaluation of performance of the participants in the OPs of the ASCs. These are; presentation by participants; continuous evaluation; on the basis of their day to day behavior; and pre-test/post-test evaluation.

Table- 9.3: Evaluation of Performance of the Participants

SOPQ: How performance of participants is evaluated?	f	%
(a) Written assignments for submission	18	75
(b) Written examination	06	25
(c) Objective Tests	11	45.83
(d) Oral Tests	03	12.50

N = 24, but multiple responses possible

FREQUENCY OF THE EVALUATION

The responses of the staffs of the ASCs to a question pertaining to frequency of the evaluation of the OPs reveal that every sixth (16.67% presented in Table - 9.4) ASCs conduct evaluation between any two modules in the OPs; and similarly, 16.67% also reveal that evaluation is done at the end of each module; every second ASCs (50%) use evaluation at the end of the course; while every sixth (16.67%) use continuous evaluation in the OPs.

Table - 9.4: Frequency of the Evaluation

SOPQ: What is the frequency of the evaluation used by your ASC?	f	%
(a) Between any two modules	04	16.67
(b) At the end of each module	04	16.67
(c) At the end of the course	12	50
(d) Continuous	04	16.67

N = 24

Thus, the ASCs, which do not have any system of continuous assessment of participants' progress, must understand the importance of formative evaluation for the benefit of teacher participants. Knowledge of correct results would act as a reinforcement to motivate the teachers to do better. Similarly, the correct knowledge of the mistakes committed may guide the teachers to rectify them. Since 75% ASCs use written assignments to evaluate the performance of the participants, it is strongly recommended that assignments should not only be designed to yield valid and reliable measures to assess participants' progress, but also be commented in such a way that they act as guidelines to improve and facilitate learning. This would ensure formative evaluation of the participants and provide constructive feedback both to the participants and course coordinators, as to how well the course is being received by the participants.

CHAPTER-X

Problems of the Academic Staff Colleges

In this Chapter, the problems of the ASCs relating to core staffs, participants, resource persons, course content, methodology, reading materials, infrastructure facilities, and finance, have been surveyed. Thereafter, an attempt has been made to evaluate the inherent problems of the ASCs in the light of director and course coordinators' observations and theoretical thinking in this regard.

PROBLEMS IN RELATION TO CORE STAFF

In order to study the problems which ASCs. had faced relating to core staff, a list of three possible problems was given to the directors and the staff of the sampled institutions (see Table - 10.1). They were asked to tick mark if the given problem was applicable in their case. On the basis of judgments based on the observations and pulling of frequencies, it became possible to calculate their percentage.

From the results shown in Table - 10.1, it becomes clear that 17 (70.83%) respondents report that the core staff provided by the University Grants Commission (U.G.C.) is insufficient to run the colleges; whereas only 7 (29.17%) believe that they do not find any problem in relation to the staff provided by the U.G.C. However, it is encouraging to note that 83.33% respondents state that the concerned universities of these ASCs in India come forward to supplement the staff to overcome the hardship arising out of insufficient staff provided by the Commission. Similarly, in case of 29.17% of the respondents, it is difficult to get suitable core staff for their ASCs. This is an important area for research as it has important implications for finding out the reasons of not getting suitable core staff by these ASCs.

Table —10.1: Problems faced by the ASCs as Perceived by the Staff

Question: Which of the following problems relating to the Core Staff is faced by your ASCs?	Yes		No	
	f	%	f	%
1. Core Staff provided by the U.G.C. is insufficient	17	70.82	0	29.17
2. University provides supplementary staff to overcome this hardship	20	83.33	04	16.67
3. Difficult to get suitable core staff	07	29.17	17	70.83

N = 24

PROBLEMS RELATING TO PARTICIPANTS

With an intention to find out the problems faced by the ASCs pertaining to the participants, a list of eight possible problems was placed before the staff actually involved in the orientation programmes. They were asked to put a tick mark against the problem they perceived to be present with organizing orientation programmes. The results of the findings presented in Table - 10.2 indicate that 75% of the respondents report that the participants continue to complain about not being relieved from their respective colleges/departments in time; 95.83% staff members state that in the absence of sanction of funds for the hostel, inadequate residential facilities are provided. 83.33% respondents are of the view that the teachers who attend the orientation courses differ in their qualification, experiences and background knowledge resulting in disparity in their level of assimilation. Similarly, in the case of 29.17% staff members, the catchment areas demarcated by the U.G.C. is limited; 25% staff in order to avoid writing an assignment/project/

seminar paper, develop a tendency to choose ASCs where such requirements are not compulsory. Moreover, it is unfortunate to observe that 83.33% respondents state that some of the participants lack sufficient motivation for under-going OPs due to lack of physical facilities, 79.17% staff report that more than 40 participants cannot be selected by them at a time Thus, in general it appears that a good majority of ASCs experience lot of problems pertaining to participants selected for undergoing OPs. Which are these colleges? Why the parent departments do not relieve their teachers in time even after being permitted by their respective authorities for undergoing such programmes? Who are those participants who lack motivation in retaining themselves? These are few important questions for further research, as their empirical answers will provide the basis for quality improvement of OPs in the country.

Table- 10.2: Problems Pertaining to Participants

Question: Which of the following problems pertaining to participants of the OPs are found by your ASC?	Yes		No	
	f	%	f	%
1. The participants continue to complain about their not being relieved from their respective colleges/ departments in time	18	75	06	25
2. In the absence of sanction of funds for the hostel, inadequate residential facilities are provided	23	95.83	01	4.17
3. The teachers who attend the OPs differ in their qualifications, experiences and background knowledge. So their level of assimilation is not the same	20	83.33	04	16.67
4. The catchment area demarcated by the U.G.C. is limited	07	29.17	17	70.83

5.	Behaviour and attentiveness of certain participants is not satisfactory	12	50	12	50.00
6.	Participants in order to avoid writing an assignment/project, seminar paper, develop a tendency to choose ASCs where such requirements are not compulsory	06	25	18	75.00
7.	Some of the participants lack sufficient motivation	20	83.33	04	16.67
8.	Due to lack of physical facilities more than 40 participants cannot be selected at a time	19	79.17	05	20.83

N = 24

PROBLEMS PERTAINING TO RESOURCE PERSONS

The staffs of the ASCs were asked a question as to what problems do they find with regard to resource persons invited for OPs. There were six possible problems. The responses to these questions indicate that in 25% cases, it is difficult to get nationally reputed resource persons; in 33.33% cases, no incidentals are paid to the external resource persons; in 33.33% cases also, external resource persons feel difficulty in meeting the expenses by the daily allowances which are presently allowed by the universities; and in 83.33% cases, remuneration given to the resource persons per lecture is too meager. Similarly, it is discouraging to note that in 95.83% cases the resource persons do not provide synopsis/handouts of their lectures and in 70.83% cases, they do not use available educational gadgets for instructional purposes.

Table - 10.3: Problems Pertaining to Resource Persons

Question: Which of the following problems pertaining to resource persons of the OPs is faced by your ASCs?	Yes		No	
	f	%	f	%
1. Difficult to get nationally reputed resource persons	06	25	18	75
2. No incidentals are admissible to the external resource persons	08	33.33	16	66.67
3. External resource persons feel difficulty in meeting the expenses by the daily allowances which are presently allowed by the university	08	33.33	16	66.67
4. Some of the resource persons do not provide synopsis/handouts of their lectures	23	95.83	01	4.17
5. Some of the resource persons do not use available Educational Technology	17	70.83	07	29.17
6. Remuneration given to the resource persons per lecture is too meager	20	83.33	04	16.67

N = 24

PROBLEMS PERTAINING TO THE COURSE CONTENT

With regard to the problems relating to the course contents of the OPs, 20.83% staffs state that the course contents devised by the U.G.C. do not maintain a sound balance between academic and socio-cultural activities (See Table - 10.4). Similarly, in case of 33.33% respondents, when participants are sent to the respective parent departments for subject upgradation at times it becomes a failure. It also appears from Table -10.4 that only 4.17%, 16.67%, and 16.67% respondents report that the course contents devised by the U.G.C.

do not provide flexibility in their structure; problems are faced in developing and modifying course contents according to the availability of the subject experts and change of curriculum from one course to another according to the needs of the participants, respectively. However, on the basis of these findings it is clear that on the whole ASCs do not face major problems relating to the course contents offered to the participants in the OPs

Table - 10.4: Problems Pertaining to the Course Contents

Question: Which of the following problems pertaining to the course contents are faced by your ASC?	Yes		No	
	f	%	f	%
1. The various components of the course content suggested by the U.G.C. do not maintain a sound balance between academic and socio-cultural activities	05	20.83	19	79.17
2. When participants are sent to the respective parent departments for subject up gradation at times it becomes a failure	08	33.33	16	66.67
3. The course content devised by the U.G.C. does not provide flexibility in its structure	01	4.17	23	95.83
4. We face a lot of difficulties in modifying and developing course contents according to the availability of the subject experts	04	16.67	20	83.33
5. Difficult to change curriculum from one course to another according to the needs of participants	04	16.67	20	83.33

N = 24

PROBLEMS PERTAINING TO METHODOLOGY

With regard to the methodologies adopted in the OPs, the results presented in Table-10.5 indicate that 50% of the staff observes that the methodology used by one ASC is not made available to the others for mutual benefits. Similarly, 33.33% respondents state that due to language problems interaction between the participants and resource persons becomes very passive and a very low percentage of staff members (8.33%) believe that the use of methodology is left to the resource persons on how to deal with the topics given to them. Thus, it appears that staff members want that the methodology used by one ASC should be made available to others for mutual benefits and passive interactions arising due to language problems need further research for the effective organization of the OPs.

Table - 10.5: Problems Pertaining to Methodology

Question: Which of the following problems pertaining to the methodology adopted in the OPs are faced by your ASC?	Yes		No	
	f	%	f	%
1. The methodology used by one ASC is not available to the others for mutual benefits	12	50	12	50
2. It is often found that participants have a passive interaction with the resource persons due to language problems	08	33.33	16	66.67
3. The use of methodology is left to the resource persons on how to deal with topics given to them	16	88.89	02	8.33

N = 24

PROBLEMS PERTAINING TO READING MATERIALS

In order to ascertain the problems faced by the ASCs in relation to reading materials, a list of eight possible problems was placed before the staff members and were asked to put a tick mark against them they perceived to be associated with the reading materials. The results of the findings presented in Table - 10.6 indicate that 87.50% of the respondents report that due to increase in the price of the books it is not possible to supply adequate reading materials to the participants. Identifying suitable and relevant literature pertaining to the course content is difficult in the case of 33.33% staff members. As regards the provision for distribution of lecture notes to the participants 50% respondents state that sufficient funds are not made available for this purpose. Similarly, 66.67% and 79.17% staffs members indicate that reading materials supplied to the participants are insufficient and production of standard reading materials by the ASCs for the OPs are yet to be made, respectively. With regard to the grants sanctioned by the U.G.C. for supplying reading materials to the participants, 70.83% respondents feel that the amount is too meager to meet the expenditure against reading materials. Moreover, 91.67% and 20.83% staffs of the ASCs observe that lecture notes are not given by some resource persons and suitable, and relevant books/literature are also not always available in some thrust areas, respectively.

Thus, it appears that almost all the ASCs in India are having serious problems with regard to the reading materials supplied to their participants undergoing OPs. Whatever may be the reasons, this is an important area for research, as it would provide empirical answers for improving the quality and suitability of the reading materials.

Table- 10.6: Problems Pertaining to Reading Materials

Question: Which of the following problems pertaining to reading materials of the OPs is faced by your institution?	Yes		No	
	f	%	f	%
1. It is not possible to give adequate reading materials to the participants due to increase in the price of the books	21	87.50	03	12.50
2. It is difficult to identify suitable and relevant literature pertaining to the course content of the ASC	08	33.33	16	66.67
3. Sufficient grants are not made available for Xerox and cyclostyling of lecture notes of resource persons for distribution to participants	12	50	12	50
4. The reading materials supplied to the participants are insufficient	16	66.67	08	33.33
5. Production of standard reading materials for the OPs are yet to be made	19	79.17	05	20.83
6. The amount sanctioned by the U.G.C. for supplying reading materials to the participants is not sufficient	17	70.83	07	29.17
7. Lecture notes are not given by some resource persons	22	91.67	02	8.33
8. Suitable books and other relevant literatures are not always available in some thrust areas	05	20.83	19	79.17

N = 24

PROBLEMS RELATING TO INFRASTRUCTURE FACILITIES

An inquiry into the problems relating to infrastructure facilities of the ASCs was made through a question which had five parts relating to guest house accommodation, transport facilities, physical facilities in terms of space, building, furniture, audiovisual equipments and core staffs. The results pertaining to guest house accommodation presented in Table -10.7 reveal that 20.83% respondents report that no guest house accommodation is available for resource persons in their ASCs. In these colleges the picture of transport facilities too, is gloomy, as 75% staff members report that they do not have an independent vehicle to meet the transport requirements of the resource persons and the teacher participants. It is quite surprising to note that even today all the ASCs suffer from acute space problems both in terms of office works and accommodation as reported by 100% staff members. Similarly, 75% and 29.17% respondents state that their colleges do not have buildings of their own and even sufficient furniture cannot be purchased as per their requirements due to budgetary problems, respectively. The facilities of audiovisual aids including computers are provided only by 33.33% ASCs and 66.67% are yet to be equipped with such equipments. Moreover, the post of reader or lecturer created by U.G.C. for the smooth functioning of the ASCs, have not yet been filled up as reported by 88.33% staff members.

On the whole, it is unfortunate to observe that almost all the ASCs in India suffer from inadequate infrastructure facilities for organizing OPs. This is a serious finding, which implies that there is a lot of scope for providing facilities, and improving the functioning of the ASCs.

Table - 10.7: Problems Relating to Infrastructure Facilities

Question: Which of the following problems relating to infrastructure is faced by your ASC?	Yes		No	
	f	%	f	%
1. No guest house accommodation is available for resource persons	05	20.83	19	79.17
2. We do not have independent vehicle to meet the transport requirements of the resource persons and the teacher participants	18	75	06	25
3. We have acute space problems both in terms of office works and accommodation for teacher participants	24	100	0	0
4. Our college does not have a building of its own	18	75	06	25
5. Sufficient furniture cannot be purchased as per requirements due to present budget limitations	07	29.17	17	70.83
6. The educational technology cell of our college is not fully equipped with the necessary audiovisual aids. computer and similar equipments	16	66.67	08	33.33
7. The posts of reader or lecturer have not yet been filled up so far	20	83.33	04	16.67

N = 24

PROBLEMS RELATING TO FINANCE

As regards the financial problems of the ASCs relating to organizing OPs, data in Table - 10.8 reveals that as many as 70.83% staff members feel that due to domestic cut in the maintenance grants, the universities find it difficult to advance adequate money for the proper running of the OPs. Similarly, the grants sanctioned by the U.G.C. against various heads are inadequate, observed by 70.83% respondents. It is surprising to note that the U.G.C. which has been funding the ASCs since 1987 does not release the grants to various ASCs in time, report 66.67% staff members, 33.33% feel that due to some inaccurate statements of account submitted by the university, the U.G.C. does not release the money to the ASCs. In order to check this type of irregularities, 75% respondents feel that the financial matters be handled by the Director's office rather than the routine office activities of the university office. Moreover, 50% respondents report that no specific funds are made available to the ASCs for the purchase of furniture, stationires etc. both for the office and hostels. It is hard to believe, although the response is very less, that 4.17% staff members indicate that the grants received by the university from the U.G.C. are not released by the university to the ASCs in time causing postponement of the OPs. Thus, it is seen that most of the ASCs in India suffer from financial constraints. Hence concerted efforts, both at the university and the U.G.C. levels should be made to help strengthen the financial positions of the ASCs, sooner the better.

Table- 10.8: Problems Relating to Finance

Question: Which of the following problems relating to the finance of the OPs are faced by your ASC?	Yes		No	
	f	%	f	%
1. Due to domestic cuts in the maintenance grants, the university has been finding it difficult to advance adequate money for the proper running of the course	17	70.83	07	29.17
2. Grants sanctioned by the U.G.C. against various heads are inadequate	17	70.83	07	29.17
3. The U.G.C. does not release the grants in time	16	66.67	8	33.33

4. Due to the inaccurate statement of accounts submitted by the universities the money is not released to the ASCs	08	33.33	16	66.67
5. Financial matters to be handled by the Director's office need to be delinked from routine office activities of the university office	18	75	06	25.00
6. No specific funds are made available for furniture, stationeries etc.	12	50	12	50.00
7. The grants received by the university from the U.G.C. are not released by the university to the ASC in time causing postponement of the programmes	01	4.17	23	95.83

N = 24

It is evident from the findings of the study that the systems adopted for the orientation of the university and college teachers by the ASCs in India suffer from numerous problems. There are several indicators to this effect. For example, a majority of the staff members, actually involved in the ASCs, have perceived the OPs as lacking sufficient core-staff, adequate hostel and residential facilities and sufficient motivation on the part of the participants. The resource persons invited to conduct the OPs are not serious in providing lecture handouts and in using audiovisual aids to support their lectures. The OPs fail to arouse active interaction between the resource persons and participants as most of the resource persons believe in the traditional rituals of delivering lectures. ASCs all over the country fail to provide adequate reading materials to their participants either due to increase in the price of the books or no attempts have, so far, been made by them to produce standard reading materials. Due to irregularities in release and utilization of funds by the concerned authorities some of the staff colleges are forced to postpone their scheduled OPs. Moreover, a majority of staff members involved in organizing OPs all over the country feel that due to acute problems of space, buildings, conveyance and vacancy of the posts of core staffs for quite sometimes now, OPs have to some extent, failed to achieve their intended goals.

Thus, it is hoped that this study would assist and stimulate policy-planners and university administrators concerned with the professional orientations of university and college teachers to re-think and re-plan the system adopted for this purpose in the future so that the ASCs in the country overcome the above mentioned pitfalls and achieve their avowed objectives.

CHAPTER-XI

FUTURE PLANS

With regard to the future plans for the improvement of the OPs, 1166.67 college and university teachers have been proposed to be covered in the next five years with an average of 233.33 teachers per year by each ASC. Each ASC has proposed 27.5 OPs to be organized in the next five years with a plan of organizing 5.5 OPs per year on an average (See Table - 11.1). Thus it reflects that each ASC wants to give orientation about 40 teachers on an average in one module. Moreover, it is encouraging to note that the ASCs intend to organize a sufficient number of OPs in the future with a reasonable intake, thus fulfilling the aspirations of the UGC that an ASC should organize up to five OPs with 40-50 newly recruited teachers in each module.

Table - 11.1: Numbers of Teachers to be Covered and OPs to be Organised

Q: Please furnish the number of teachers to be covered and OPs proposed to be organized in the next five years.		Total	Average	
			Five Years	Per Years
(a)	No. of Teachers	14000	1166.67	233.33
(b)	No. of OPs	330	27.50	5.50

N=12

THRUST AREAS OF THE OPs FOR FUTURE PLANNING

The staffs of the ASCs were asked to reveal their thrust areas to be covered for future planning of the OPs. For this purpose they were provided with three areas to respond with an opportunity to add more areas if they intended. The responses to this question indicate that for 79.17% cases teaching techniques would be the thrust areas, 75%

staffs observe that participatory skills would be their thrust areas and for 79.17% cases also the thrust areas of the OPs for future planning would be the teacher taught interaction. Moreover, the ASCs have rightly visualized that with the continuous innovation and explosion of knowledge, teachers' role and requirements would be expanded in future. Thus apart from these, some significant areas such as computer education, quality control and improvement in higher education, value oriented education would be the thrust areas for future planning of the OPs in the ASCs as suggested by the respondents.

Table- 11.2: Thrust Areas of the OPs for Future Planning

Q. The thrust areas of the OPs would be:		f	%
(a)	Teaching Techniques	19	79.17
(b)	Participatory Skills	18	75.00
(c)	Teacher taught Interaction	19	79.17

N = 24, but multiple responses possible

FUTURE PLAN PERTAINING TO THE DEVELOPMENT OF THE STAFFS

As regards the development of the staff in future, 66.67% respondents state that one reader and one lecturer will be appointed permanently. For the better management of the ASC, 61.11% respondents state that a plan is on anvil to upgrade the post of lecturer to a reader in the future.

Table - 11.3: Future Plans for the Development of the Staff

Q. Your future plans about the development of the staff	Yes		No	
	f	%	f	%
(a) One reader and one lecturer will be appointed permanently	18	66.67	06	33.33
(b) The post of lecturer will be upgraded to a reader for the better management of the ASC	17	61.11	07	38.89

N = 24, but multiple responses possible

FUTURE PLANS RELATING TO THE COURSE CONTENTS

The staffs of the ASCs were asked about the future plans in developing course contents for OPs. Total eight possible areas were provided to them and they were asked to tick the area, which they found suitable to be included in the course content of the OPs. The results presented in the Table - 11.4 have shown that 91.67% respondents intend that different topics relevant to higher education, research methodology and innovations will be incorporated in the course contents and topics covering latest thinking in subjects concerned will be added (79.17%). Similarly, 79.17% respondents also reveal that topics relating to classroom management will be incorporated. 70.83% of the respondents observe that the third component i.e. Subject Up gradation will be conducted at ASC premises for bringing about more seriousness. Moreover, 66.67% of respondents have the plan that the entire course content will be revised on the basis of suggestions from the experts as well as the participants to meet the contemporary needs. But it is to note that half of the respondents i.e. 50% have a plan for regular meetings of the course co-ordinators for suggesting changes in the course contents on the basis of their experiences. 66.67% of the staff states that extension education will receive more attention in the future and the application of knowledge transfer of technology will be given more priority (79.17%). Thus it may be concluded that ASCs have adequate future plans to make the course content up to date and purposeful for the OPs.

Table - 11.4: Future Plans Pertaining to Development of the Course Content

Q. Your future plans about the development of the course content.	f	%
(a) Different topics relevant to higher education, research methodology, and innovations will be incorporated in the course content	22	91.67
(b) Topics covering latest thinking in subjects concerned will be added	19	79.17

(c) Topics relating to classroom management will be incorporated	19	79.17
(d) The third component, i.e. subject upgradation will be conducted at ASC premises for bringing about more seriousness	17	70.83
(e) The entire course content will be revised on the basis of suggestions from the experts as well as the participants to meet the contemporary needs	16	66.67
(f) Regular meetings of the course coordinators will be organized to suggest changes in the course content on the basis of their experiences	12	50.00
(g) Extension education will receive more attention in the future	16	66.67
(h) The application of knowledge transfer of technology will be given more priority	19	79.17

N = 24, but multiple responses possible

FUTURE PLANS PERTAINING TO METHODOLOGY

As regards the future plans pertaining to the methodology to be adopted in the OPs, the results in the Table - 11.5 indicate that 91.67% respondents observe that more and more importance will be given to interaction rather than lecture method. Same number of respondents also state that more and more seminars and participants' presentation will be arranged and group discussions will be encouraged. However, 66.67% staffs report that one day in every week will be devoted to a discussion among the participants themselves on an assigned theme from within the component. 79.17% respondents intend to arrange field trips and on the spot lectures more frequently, 75% respondents observe that importance will be given to the use of audio visual techniques including computer -aided instruction and programmed instruction in future. Moreover, in 79.17% cases methodology used by one staff college will be made available to others for mutual benefits, 83.33% staff of the ASCs will give more importance to brainstorming sessions, assignments etc. But it is discouraging to note that only half of the staff of the ASCs i.e. 50% would give importance to experimental progrmmes. In other words, it indicates that 50% staffs of the ASCs are reluctant to involve themselves in innovating teaching methodologies. What might be the reasons behind their reluctance to adopt innovative practices? Who are those 50% staff and what are their motivations? All these questions call for further investigations in this area of work.

Table - 11.5: Future Plans about Methodology

Q.	Your future Plans about Methodology adopted in the OPs	f	%
(a)	More and more importance will be given to interaction rather than lecture method.	22	91.67
(b)	More and more seminars and participants presentations will be arranged and group discussion will be encouraged	22	91.67
(c)	One day each in every week will be devoted to a discussion among the participants themselves on an assigned theme within the component	16	66.67
(d)	Field trips and on the spot lectures will be more frequently arranged	19	79.17
(e)	Use of audio-visual techniques including computer aided instruction and programmed instruction will be given more importance	18	75.00
(f)	Methodology used by one staff college should be made available to others for mutual benefits	19	79.17
(g)	More importance will be given to brainstorming sessions assignments, etc.	20	83.33
(h)	Experimental programmes will be greatly emphasized	12	50.00

N = 24, but multiple responses possible

FUTURE PLANS RELATING TO THE DEVELOPMENT OF READING MATERIALS

With an intention to study the future plans relating to the development of reading materials for the OPs, the staffs of the ASCs were asked to respond to eight different aspects of the reading materials. The results presented in the Table -11.6 reveal that 87.50% respondents state that prompt services will be given to resource persons in preparing of their topics. 87.50% respondents also state that the UGC should enhance the amount for providing adequate reading materials to the participants and 83.33% staff will identify literatures pertaining to the course content of the ASC. Similarly, 70.83% respondents would open documentary section in future for the ready reference of the participants and going beyond that 83.33% respondents state that ASC news letter will be launched and be made a monthly feature. 70.83% staffs observe that reading materials on 'Seminar Reading' will be published in due course on different areas of the OP. It was encouraging to note that 66.67% respondents state that a comprehensive core reading material may be prepared inviting papers from eminent resource persons in the field covering all the four components of the curriculum of the OP and be distributed to the participants at the beginning of the course itself. But only 50% respondents are of the view that besides the library of the ASC the library facilities of the university and other local colleges may be made available to the participants during the course.

Table- 11.6: Future Plans about the Development of Reading Materials

Q.	Your future plans about the development of the reading materials of the OPs	f	%
(a)	Prompt service will be given to resource persons in preparing their topics.	21	87.50
(b)	The UGC should enhance the amount to provide adequate reading materials to the participants	21	87.50
(c)	Literature pertaining to the course content of the ASC will be identified	20	83.33

(d) Documentation section will be opened for the ready reference of the participants	17	70.83
(e) ASC news letter will be launched and be made monthly feature.	20	83.33
(f) Reading materials on 'seminar reading' will be published in due course in different areas of the OP.	17	70.83
(g) A comprehensive core reading material may be prepared inviting papers from eminent resource persons in the field covering all the four components of the curriculum of the OP and be distributed to the participants at the beginning of the course itself	16	66.67
(h) Besides the library of the ASC, the library of the university and other local colleges may be made available to the participants during the course.	12	50.00

N = 24, but multiple responses possible

FUTURE PLANS PERTAINING TO THE DEVELOPMENT OF THE ADMINISTRATION

With reference to the development of administration, the staffs of the ASCs were asked about their future plans and accordingly they responded to a total number of nine aspects of administration of the ASC. The results shown in Table - 11.7 indicate that 58.33% respondents argue that the system of hired cocrdinators should be dispensed with. Majority of the respondents i.e. 70.83% are of the view that more senior positions at the level of readers and professors should be sanctioned by the UGC. 79.17% respondents observe that a research cell should be established and implemented as soon as possible. Most of the respondents i.e. 91.67% report that the UGC should clarify the position of the Director within the university system and the universities be asked to confer the membership of the Academic Council, Executive Council and the Court upon the Director. 75% respondents reveal that a senior position in accounts in the staff college should be sanctioned by the UGC. 79.17% state that the ASC should have a separate building of its own for its smooth functioning. Moreover, 83.33% staffs state that the Director of the staff college should have some discretionary power to take decision to run the programmes effectively. 87.50% respondents argue that the ASC should have autonomy in its functioning and 79.17% respondents want that more staff should be appointed to run the staff college effectively. Thus it implies that the ASCs are looking forward to the development of the administration of the ASCs so as to run the programmes effectively.

Table - 11.7: Future Plans about the Improvement of the Administration

Q. Your future plans about the development of the administration of the OPs.	f	%
(a) The system of hired coordinators should be dispensed with.	14	58.33
(b) More senior positions at the level of Readers and Professors should be sanctioned by the UGC	17	70.83
(c) A research cell should be established and implemented as soon as possible.	19	79.17
(d) The UGC should clarify the position of the Director within the university system and the universities be asked to confer the membership of the Academic Council, Executive Council (Syndicate) and the Court (Senate) upon the Director.	22	91.67
(e) A senior position in accounts in the staff college should be sanctioned by the UGC.	18	75.00
(f) The ASC should have a separate building of its own for its smooth functioning.	19	79.17
(g) The Director of the Staff College should have some discretionary power to take decision to run the programmes effectively.	20	83.33
(h) The ASC should have autonomy in its functioning	21	87.50
(i) More staff should be appointed to run the staff college effectively.	19	79.17

N = 24, but multiple responses possible

FUTURE PLANS PERTAINING TO FINANCE

With regard to future plans of the ASCs pertaining to the financial aspect of the OPs, 91.67% staffs of the ASCs state that grants for books and equipments should be enhanced and such grants should be given to the ASCs not on early basis but for whole plan period. Similarly, 87.50% staff unanimously advocate for providing a separate grant for the ASCs to bring out their own journals. Majority of the respondents i.e.83.33% report that specific funds should be sanctioned for furniture and stationeries. Similarly, 83.33% respondents state that provision should be made on per participant basis for their lodging arrangement until a separate building for college/hostel is constructed. A similar number of respondents (83.33%) also argue that funds should be provided for purchasing of vehicle in place of the present hired one. Moreover, in 91.67% cases timely release of the grants by the UGC is essential. In 79.17% cases the Directors should be given full autonomy to utilize the funds to avoid undue delay in implementing the programmes and plans of the ASCs. A similar number of respondents (79.17%) argue for providing cent percent assistance by the UGC for all the future programmes on short term and long term basis. However, 83.33% respondents express their opinion that a substantial portion of the unassigned grants allotted to the university may be diverted to the ASC fund for conducting workshops for principals and heads of university departments. On the other hand, 75% respondents are of the view that separate funds may be specifically allotted for such courses. Moreover, as many as 87.50% staffs state that amount under working expenses may be raised up to Rs.4 lakhs per annum. As a whole, it indicates that for better running and effective management of the ASC in general and for organizing Ops in particular a huge amount of money will be required in the future and hence the ASCs would expect regular and timely financial assistance from the UGC.

Table - 11.8: Future Plans Pertaining to the Financial Aspects of the OPs

Q. Your future plans about the development of the financial aspect of the OPs.	f	%
(a) Grants for books and equipments should be enhanced	22	91.67
(b) A separate grant should be provided for the ASCs to bring out their own journals.	21	87.50
(c) Specific funds should be sanctioned for furniture and stationeries.	20	83.33
(d) Provision should be made on per participant basis for the lodging arrangement of the participants till a separate building for college/hostel is constructed.	20	83.33
(e) Funds should be provided for purchase of vehicles in the place of the present hired one.	20	83.33
(f) Timely release of the grants by the UGC is absolutely essential	22	91.67
(g) The Director should be given full autonomy to utilize the funds to avoid undue delay in implementing the programmers and plans of the OPs.	19	79.17
(h) The UGC should provide cent percent assistance for all the future programmes on short term and long term basis.	19	79.17
(i) A substantial portion of the unassigned grants allotted to the university may be diverted to the ASC fund for conducting workshop for principals and heads of university departments.	20	83.33
(j) Otherwise, separate funds may be specially allotted for such courses.	18	75.00
(k) Amount under working expenses may be raised up to Rs. 4 lakhs per annum.	21	87.50

N = 24, but multiple responses possible.

FUTURE PLANS RELATING TO THE IMPROVEMENT OF EVALUATION

An enquiry into the future plans relating to the improvement of evaluation procedure of the OPs was made under question No.9 that had several dimensions. The results in Table-11.9 show that 83.33% respondents observe that in order to assess the effectiveness of the programme, participants who have attended the course should again be invited for a few days seminar to know as to how far their participation has helped them in performing their jobs. Majority of the respondents (54.17%) argue that there should be written examination at the end of each course. A good number of respondents (79.17%) state that participants will be required to give their reactions to different aspects of the programmes at the end of each course. Most of the respondents (83.33) observe that self-evaluation of the participants through a checklist should be carried out. It is encouraging to observe that almost all the ASCs in India have substantially improved their evaluation procedures by adopting the above-mentioned measures.

Table - 11.9: Future Plans about the Improvement of Evaluation

	Q. Your future plans about the improvement of evaluation of the OPs.	f	%
(a)	In order to assess the effectiveness of the programme, participants who have attended the course should again be invited for a few days seminar to know as to how far their participation has helped in performance of their jobs	20	83.33
(b)	There should be written examination at the end of the each course.	13	54.17
(c)	Participants will be required to give their reactions to different aspects of the programme at the end of the each course.	19	79.17
(d)	Self- evaluation of participants through a check list will be carried out.	20	83.33

N = 24, but multiple responses possible.

CHAPTER-XII

MAJOR FINDINGS AND SUGGESTIONS

A. SELECTION OF PARTICIPANTS

1. The study reveals that no uniformity is being maintained by the ASCs in India in terms of intake of one OP. However, it is reasonable to observe that the intake capacity among the ASCs falls within 30 - 50 participants in one OP.

2. Almost all ASCs in India (95.83%) follow strict criteria in the selection of teachers for the OP.

3. Out of 24 staffs of the ASCs in India, 66.67%, 62.5%, 37.5%, 20.83% and 4.17% of them invite a list of the fresh teachers in university/college from the catchments areas, from outside catchment areas, only those teachers who are appointed on substantive posts, teachers from selected subjects and educational administrators for the OPs, respectively.

4. Almost all ASCs in India (91.88%) strictly follow the UGC norms for selection of participants for the OPs.

5. Most of the ASCs in India (83.33%) reveal that the catchment area demarcated by the UGC for inviting participants is sufficient.

6. 79.17% of the ASCs in India stipulate a minimum period between successive courses for selection to the OPs. Moreover, ASCs also stipulate an approximate period

ranging from 10 months to 2 years between successive courses for selection to the OPs.

7. Most of the staffs of the ASCs in India (75%) think that the participants selected by the ASC for a given course attend the same as expected. However, 25% of them think the same negatively and reveal the reasons that principals/heads of the institutions do not release the teachers in time and observe that some of the teachers lack sufficient motivation to attend the OPs.

B. COURSE CONTENT AND COURSE MATERIALS

1. Almost all the ASCs in India (95.83%) invariably follow the course components devised by the UGC for realization of aims of higher education.

2. However, the study further reveals that with regard to the academic standard of the course content offered by the ASCs in India, 50.07% and 62.88% of participants sometimes find the course content of having academic standard and interesting, respectively.

3. With regard to the course materials supplied by the ASCs in the Ops, out of 765 participants responded, 61.83% of them were satisfied with the course materials supplied to them during the Ops. However, 34.77% of participants were dissatisfied with the same, because they opined that course materials supplied were irrelevant and obsolete.

C. DURATION AND ORGANISATION OF THE COURSE

1. As regards the duration of the Orientation Programme, almost all the ASCs in India (91.66%) follow the UGC rules of 28 days Op.

2. Out of 765 participants, a good majority of them (78.95%) perceive that present duration of 4 weeks Op is quite sufficient. Moreover, of those who oppose the same, 10.98% and 9.54% of participants suggest that duration of the OP should be less than 4 weeks (1 to 3

weeks) and more than 4 weeks (5 to 12 weeks), respectively.

3. All the ASCs in India (100%) organize OPs exclusively of interdisciplinary nature. Further, 41.67%, 29.17%, 20.83% and 8.83% of Ops of ASCs include 6 to 7 disciplines, more than 7 disciplines, 5 to 6 disciplines and 4 to 5 disciplines at a time in order of the response rate, respectively.

4. Out of 765 participants, 71.50% of them find worthfulness of the time and money spent in attending the OPs. However, 22.35% of participants find worthless to spend time and money in attending the Ops.

D. CO-CURRICULAR AND FINANCIAL ASPECTS OF THE OP

1. Out of 765 participants, most of them (82.22%) think that some co-curricular activities are essential in the OPs. Only 15.69% of participants think the same not essential in the OPs.

2. Majority of the participants (48.76%) are satisfied with the co-curricular activities offered in the OPs. 43.53% of participants are not satisfied with the same; and they suggest for pre-planning of co-curricular programmes and availability of the facilities for the activities in the ASCs.

3. 60.00% of participants are satisfied with the financial aspects of the OPs and the same is not satisfactory to 32.16% participants.

E. RESOURCE PERSONS AND THEIR BACK GROUND RELEVANT TO THE CONTENT

1. In most of the ASCs (58.33%), resource persons invited for the OPs are both external and internal. However, 29.17% and 12.50% of ASCs invite exclusively internal and local resource persons, and external resource persons for the OPs, respectively.

2. With regard to the selection criteria of resource persons, as many as 91.67% of the ASCs take into account the participants feedback while selecting resource persons for the OPs. However, both scholarship and teachership, subject/area specialization is also taken into account in 79.17% cases while selecting the resource persons.

3. Out of 765 participants, most of them (75.95%) are satisfied with the resource persons and their background relevant to the content of the course. However, 21.96% of participants are not satisfied with the same; and suggest inviting competent and devoted teachers (experts), renowned persons from other universities as resource persons.

F. METHODS OF PRESENTATION

1. Most of the ASCs in India (87.5%) largely adopt lecture-cum group discussion and lecture-cum discussion-cum seminar methods for delivering course content in the OPs. Moreover, in order of response rate, 79.17%, 70.89%, 66.67%, 33.33% and 27.17% ASCs adopt book reviews and paper presentations, field visits; studies; surveys; assignments and microteaching sessions; lecture-cum demonstration and brainstorming; lecture-cum group discussion-cum seminar and symposia/workshops; self-study; and role play/games in delivering the course content in the Ops, respectively.

2. Almost all ASCs (95.83%) have made paper presentation compulsory. Other compulsory methodologies adopted for delivering the course content in the OPs are assignments (66.67%), book reviews (54.17%) and micro-teaching sessions (45.83%).

3. Out of 765, 69.15% of participants are satisfied with the methods adopted for the presentation of the course content in the OPs. The same is not satisfactory to 26.14% participants, and they opine that more visual

demonstrations, field visits; workshops, assignments, role play/games, etc. are required to be adopted in the Ops.

G. MEDIA AND AIDS USED

1. With regard to the media and aids used in the OPs, Overhead Projector, TV and VCR, Slide Projector, Computer and Educational Films are used by 95.83%, 79.17%, 87.50% and 70.83% ASCs in India, respectively.

2. Participants under investigation rank 1, 2, 3, 4 and 5 to Overhead Projector, Slide Projector, TV and VCR, Computer and Educational Films on the basis of their frequency of use in delivering the course content of the Ops, respectively.

3. Out of 765 participants, 62,48% are satisfied with the media and aids used for the presentation of the course content in the OPs. However, 33.99% of participants are not satisfied, and hence suggest that computer/ internet, educational films/documents, etc. should be used.

H. INTERACTION TO PARTICIPANTS OFFERED

1. In most of the ASCs in India (83.33%), the mode of interaction between the participants and the resource persons is exchange of views/ideas between the participants and resource persons, and paper presentation/seminar. Moreover, group discussion is offered by 79.17% ASCs in India for ensuring interaction between participants and the resource persons.

2. Participants under investigation rank 1, 2, 3, 4 and 5 to exchange of views/ideas between the participants and resource persons, group-discussion, paper presentation/ seminar, compulsory question-answer session and book review on the basis of the process of interaction among the participants and resource persons while undergoing OPs, respectively.

3. Out of 765, most of the participants, i.e. 77.12% are satisfied with the process of interaction offered in the OPs. However, 19.48% are not satisfied with the same and hence suggest that more time should be provided for interaction in the OPs.

I. MODE OF DELIVERY

1. Most of the ASCs in India (83.33%) adopt interaction as a mode of delivery of the course content in the OPs. 70.83% of the ASCs adopt methods of presentation and use of media and aids as modes of delivery in the OPs.

2. Out of 765 participants, majority of them (66.67%) opine that more time should be given to individual interaction than delivering lecture (25.62%) during the OPs.

J. EVALUATION OF THE OPs

1. Out of 24 staff of the ASCs in India, 66.67% of them use compulsory evaluation of the course. However, in 25% cases, the ASCs use voluntary evaluation of the OPs.

2. As regards the kinds of evaluation used in the OPs of the ASCs in India, 66.676%, 62.50% and 50% ASCs use self-evaluation by participants in terms of their own perceived attitudinal charge and skill enhancement, programme evaluation by participants in terms of effectiveness of the programme, and formal evaluation of participants in terms of their achievements, respectively.

3. The ASCs in India evaluate performance of the participants in the OPs through written assignments for submission (75%), written examination (25%), objective test (45.83%) and oral test (12.50%). In addition, some other devices such as, presentation by participants, continuous evaluation, etc. are also used by the ASCs.

4. 50% of the ASCs in India use evaluation at the end of the course. However, 16.67% of them conduct

evaluation between any two modules, at the end of each module and continuously, respectively.

COMPULSORY/VOLUNTARY PARTICIPATION IN OPs

1. Out of 765 teachers, 70.33% want participation in orientation programmes to be made compulsory, whereas 29.41% want it to be voluntary.

SUITABILITY OF OPs

1. 63.53%, 29.54% and 5.49% of college and university teachers find the OPs adequate, less adequate and not adequate, respectively.
2. With regard to the quality of the OPs, 65.36%, 28.24% and 4.44% of college and university teachers find it up-to-date, not up-to-date and obsolete, respectively.
3. Out of 765 participants, 25.36% and 66.93% perceive the organized activities in the OPs most relevant and relevant, respectively. Only 6.41% find the same irrelevant.
4. Majority of college and university teachers (58.82%) find the communication of the Ops very effective. However, 38.69% and 1.57% find the same not so effective and not at all effective, respectively.

ACADEMIC VALUE OF THE OPs

1. 24 staffs of the ASCs in India state that the foremost purpose served during the OPs is that the excellence in the academic standards of the university and college teachers is promoted. Other purposes served by the ASCs in India in order of importance at second, third, fourth, fifth, sixth, seventh, eighth and ninth innovation in the area of teaching and pedagogical science, creation of awareness among the teachers about the society and environment, promotion of teachers' professional growth, encouraging teachers to relate education with national development, promotion of optimum growth of teachers personality, motivating

the teachers to evolve a philosophy of education, dissemination of knowledge and service to the society and up gradation of the knowledge of the teachers about their respective subjects, respectively.

2. As many as 88.63% university and college teachers find the OPs beneficial in terms of identifying and developing effective style of teaching, while as low as 51.76% are benefited after undergoing the OPs in terms of acquiring a lot of latest knowledge and skills. However, the university and college teachers find some additional academic values of the OPs such as imparting knowledge effectively (85.75%), making proper choice of teaching methods (82.22%), linking research with developing effective methodology of teaching (73.20%), planning and executing daily teaching lessons properly and confidently (78.43%), preparing and using teaching aids effectively (76.34%), organizing different co-curricular activities (67.98%), developing and understanding the system and role of higher education (77.91%), developing participating skills and management techniques (72.68%) and knowing and playing ones role effectively (69.23%).

COMPARISON OF COURSE COMPONENTS

As regards the objective 3 of the present study, the course contents of the sampled ASCs were collected during the field visit and have been arranged under four components. A close observation of the course content of the ASCs in India reveals that all the ASCs follow the four curriculum components devised by the UGC. They are;

(i) Component A: Awareness of Linkages between Society,Environment, Development and Education;

(ii) Component B: Philosophy of Education, Indian Education System and Pedagogy;

(iii) Component C: Subject Up gradation; and

(iv) Component D: Management and Personality Development

A comparison between course content under each component of the ASCs in India shows that more or less course contents of all the ASCs are similar. The reasons of similarity of course content among the ASCs may be attributed to the fact that all the ASCs invariably follow the same UGC guidelines as regards the course component. However, a little variation has been found in terms of the above-mentioned components:

(i) Politicisation of education, Indian constitution, society in Assam, water situation in Maharastra, role of teachers beyond the classroom, democracy in India, problems and prospects, etc. are included in the course component 'A' of different ASCs.

(ii) In the course component 'B' of some ASCs, manpower planning and higher education, teachers' autonomy, mutual health and college students' counseling, creativity and innovation in higher education, privatization of education, etc. have been incorporated.

(iii) Language teaching, the concept of teacher education, etc. are included in the course component 'C by few ASCs, and

(iv) Few ASCs in India, in the course Component 'D' include professional ethics, interpersonal effectiveness, sports/ physical fitness and its management at university level, and organisation of conferences/seminars/workshops, etc.

SUGGESTIONS FOR IMPROVEMENT

Some suggestions based on the findings of the study and observations made by the respondents may be mentioned hereunder for the improvement of OPs in India.

(i) An adequate co-ordination between college participants and the ASCs should be maintained so that teachers can attend the course in proper time.

(ii) More emphasis should be laid on teaching techniques.

(iii) Hostel accommodations should be provided to participants and every participant should stay at the hostel so that effective interaction can be established,

(iv) More emphasis should be given on research work.

(v) Participants from other states should be invited.

(vi) The UGC should supply the materials, data, etc. about the latest developments in different fields to ASCs.

(vii) Knowledge of modern Information Technology should be included.

(viii) Every university should have one ASC so that everyone can manage oneself.

(ix) Feedback should be regularly obtained to make the OP. effective,

(x) 50% of the panel of RPs should be nominated by the UGC.

(xi) Practical approach to teaching should be emphasized.

(xii) Information regarding the OPs should be made convenient to each college.

(xiii) Every University/College teacher must undergo OPs before joining in the job.

(xiv) The ASCs library should be rich enough to facilitate skill development of the participants.

(xv) RPs should be drawn from different fields like, Industry, Bank, Govt. Organisation, NGOs, Defense, UGC, etc. instead of inviting only professors from the universities who are mostly retired.

(xvi) T.A. and D.A. should be enhanced.

(xviii) Stress management techniques should be emphasized.

(xix) Medium of interaction should be English.

(xx) Professional ethics of teacher, Educational Technology, problems of youth and organization of co-curricular activities should be made compulsory subjects for OPs.

(xxi) Efficient management of OPs is required.

(xxii) The number of participants should be less (30) so that greater interaction can be ensured.

(xxiii) The expenditure for attending the OPs should be borne by the participants themselves.

(xxiv) At the end of the OP written examination on both theory and practical should be conducted to ascertain participants' gain from the course.

(xxv) Continuous evaluation of participants is essential.

(xxvi) Monitoring system to examine the impact of the OPs should be evolved.

(xxvii) The UGC should frame a rule so that the concerned authority, to attend the OPs, should release every university/college teacher, after one year of teaching.

(xxviii) The frequency of conducting Op should be increased.

(xxix) The ASC should have their own building.

CHAPTER-XIII

Teacher Education Through Distance Mode

INTRODUCTION

In the early 1987, while attempting to put the National Policy on Education (NPE) — 1986 into action, the University Grants Commission (UGC) wanted to do something about the professional orientation of the university and the college teachers. The Commission had two clear cut alternatives before it:

(i) to implement the scheme of Academic Staff College (ASC) mooted out in the Education Commission — 1966, and

(ii) to implement the recommendations of the Mehrotra Committee — 1986 and launch orientation and refresher courses through Indira Gandhi National Open University (IGNOU) by adopting Distance Education Methodology.

For reasons best known to itself, the UGC adopted the first alternative and launched the Academic Staff Orientation Scheme. It was probably due to the desire of the then Central Government to see its NPE being put into action immediately and the consequent pressure on the UGC, the UGC had no time to evolve a new model for the orientation of the university and the college teachers through distance education. Hence, the already existing model of the ASC proposed by the Education Commission was implemented. As a consequence, ASCs were established. At present, about 57 ASCs are offering regular orientation programmes to the teachers all over the country through traditional face-to-face teaching methodology. Which of the two alternatives, i.e. professional orientation through traditional face-to-face teaching or through distance education is academically more sound and economically more viable is a question that seems valid even today after the establishment of the ASCs.

The author is thoroughly convinced that, considered from the academic and economic point of view, the distance education mode, as it offers autonomy and independence in planning and executing learning, will be much more effective than the formal face-to-face teaching and learning sessions offered at the ASCs now. The economic viability of the ASCs, on the other hand, can be questioned on the following grounds related to heavy direct costs:

- Payment of TA (Travel Allowance) and DA (Dearness Allowance) to the teachers deputed for the course.
- Payment of TA and DA and honorarium to the resource persons called to deliver lectures at the ASCs.
- Establishment and maintenance costs of the ASCs.
- Teaching gets disrupted in the parent departments from which the teachers have been deputed and hence substitutes are appointed during the period of deputation of regular teachers.

Above all, the academic viability of the face-to-face sessions organised in the ASCs for the orientation of university and college teachers depends, to a great extent, on the seriousness of the teachers with which they undergo these courses. Often the seriousness seems difficult to be ensured and ascertained.

As opposed to the running of orientation courses through traditional face-to-face sessions in ASCs, distance education methodology offers a non-traditional possibility for significantly reducing the above mentioned direct and indirect costs involved in the running of orientation courses through the ASCs. Economic viability of the distance education for offering certain courses in higher education is established beyond doubt, Hence, it is proposed that to launch staff development programmes through distance education would be viable.

RATIONALE

The main purpose of having professional orientation courses for staff development is to enable teachers to have some access to academic and professional study at an advance level on a continual basis. Staff development programme thus implies widening and deepening of knowledge and insight related to the subjects and academic pursuits with which teachers are preoccupied in practising their profession. Widening of the knowledge mainly serves purposes of updating, bringing new subject matter into focus and/or including entirely a new subject in the academic and professional competence of the teachers. Deepening refers to a specialised learning that leads to higher research or aims at bettering the competence of teachers to undertake independent research.

Such a course of study aimed at widening, updating and deepening of knowledge naturally has to differ from regular university courses of study because the maturity and the intellectual level of learners are different in the two cases. This difference and the difference in the very level of study implying greater demand and standard of knowledge, academic work and problem solving characterize the orientation of university and college teachers as a study of specialized type, i.e., the one which may lead to academic excellence. It is this difference that calls for teaching and learning approaches which are different from those adopted for regular study of students at colleges and universities.

THEORETICAL CONSIDERATIONS

University and college teachers, being adults having family and other private responsibilities, cannot be treated as regular post-graduate university students. For the former the traditional face-to-face teaching method adopted in a class-room situation may not prove to be as effective as it is for the regular university students. Being adults and already having acquired post graduate degrees or above, the university and the college teachers have the capabilities to read and understand the concepts contained in a written material. What is then required is to provide these teachers opportunities to utilize their leisure time to study in order to acquire knowledge at the frontiers of new knowledge in their respective subjects/areas of specialization. Orientation through distance mode is suggested not only because of the autonomy and independence it provides to the university and college teachers without disturbing their productive works out also the general economy that it offers has attracted the attention of the author. As regards the economic viability of distance education it has been found out elsewhere that "a successful teacher training project in mathematics for some 50,000 active teachers in 1969-71 proved to require only 3% of the cost of a parallel residential study programme with equal effectiveness" (Holmberg 1973).

In the light of the above considerations, it is hypothesised that for the orientation of university and college teachers any academic programme which is based on self-learning material will prove to be more academically and economically viable than a programme which is based on traditional face-to-face teaching-learning approach.

This hypothesis is theoretically substantiated by the fact that self-learning material designed as self-contained course will prove to be academically viable for teachers because it will provide them:

(i) the possibilities for individualization of study pace, and

(ii) the possibility of experiencing the study-cum-work on their own which is felt to develop independence and lead to greater autonomy of learning than other types of study.

Further, it will prove to be economically more viable because self-learning material in the form of a self-contained course can be used as distance study material. Once this material is used as distance education material, it would offer the teachers the following economic advantages which distance education offers in general:

- The applicability of distance education to large groups of teachers as a kind of mass communication.
- The economy of both the large group approach and the elimination of the need for residential teaching or a diminished component of it enables the study to take place during leisure time anywhere without disrupting the productive work (teaching) of the teachers.

The feasibility of developing large scale projects by enlisting the services of the very best subject specialists and educationists. For example, they can be utilized to write the course materials.

PSYCHOLOGICAL CONSIDERATIONS

There are psychological bases that support the contention that learning and retention is enhanced through the study of written materials produced on the basis of certain psycho-educational theories. The strongest support for the written instructional material and its capability of influencing the learning and retention has come from the influential work of Ausubel (1968) on meaningful verbal learning and the notion of "mathemagenic behaviours" introduced by Rothkopf (1966).

Ausubel pointed out that in learning emphasis on cognitive process and structure is important. His emphasis on cognitive process and structure has shown the importance of controlling the presentation of instructional material and the influence of the knowledge that learners bring with them to the learning situation. In support of his argument Ausubel stated that "If I had to reduce all educational psychology to just one principle, I would say this: the most important single factor influencing learning is what the learner already knows. Ascertain this and teach accordingly". Thus, Ausubel's work drew attention to meaningful text learning. But it was Rothkopf who suggested that learners of specific subjects, while studying through written materials, not only learn the specific content but also acquire some general facilitative skills namely "inspection behaviours" which he later called "mathemagenic behaviours". So this notion reminds researchers that what the learner does in the learning situation is an important pointer to how much he will retain.

Based on all these conditions, the author in this chapter argues that the deliberate use of self-instructional material which will use the above psychological foundations could influence learning positively amongst university and college teachers who are adult learners.

EMPIRICAL OBSERVATIONS

Teaching through the distance mode (Self-learning material) is significantly more effective than traditional teaching in terms of better educational achievements, attitudinal changes, etc. It is not only supported by the theories of learning in general and adult learning in particular, as seated above, but is also supported by empirical researches. For instance, Das (1990) developed a package of self-learning material as a part of the course prescribed in module — II, i.e., "Science and Technology of Education" offered at the ASC, Banaras Hindu University and studied its effectiveness against traditional teaching method. The study revealed that self-learning material was significantly more effective in facilitating adult learning in terms of their achievement and attitude on criterion tests than the traditional method of teaching. Further, the experimental findings of the studies conducted in India and foreign countries by Mullick (1964), Bhusan (1973), Chauhan (1973), Govinda (1976), Sansanwal (1978), Shah (1980), Pandey (1982), Singh (1989), Sheppard (1970), Johnston and Pennypecker (1977), Lee and McLean (1978), Dean (1981), Otto (1981). Edelman (1983), Grant (1983), Neuberger (1984), and Vataravigkit (1985) related to the effectiveness of individualized instructional strategies in terms of programmed learning material, self-learning material, personalized system of instruction and mastery learning, against traditional teaching method have revealed significantly better learning outcomes in the self-learning method than traditional teaching method.

Thus, it is expected that orientation of the university and college teachers through self-learning material would result in positive transfer to new situations and deeper cognitive processing and hence better learning than traditional face-to-face teaching.

DISCUSSION

In the theoretical front we know that effective teaching occurs when active involvement of the learner in the learning process is ensured. In the traditional face-to-face teaching through lecture method, the learner's involvement in the teaching/learning process may not be active always. Because the learner may be physically involved but cognitively he may be totally absent. But in the case of self-learning material, either the learner learns, or he does not learn. He takes up the self-learning material only when he has time and is motivated to learn. The motivation in the case of self-learning material comes basically from within and is not required to be aroused by the teacher as in the case of traditional teaching although strategies to motivate the learner are used while developing the self-learning materials. Through self motivation learning is expected to be better, because while reading self-learning material the learner's (i.e. teacher's) cognitive involvement would be complete.

Further, the Academic Learning Time (ALT) for each individual is different as the learners vary in their intellectual abilities, memory, endurance for work, aptitudes and their level of educational achievement. Self-learning strategy takes this point into consideration as it allows learners to make decisions and assures responsibility for their own education. It helps learners to make decisions about what to study, when to study, how much to study and involves the learners in evaluating the effectiveness of their efforts and progress. Since this strategy makes use of clear and defined goals, promotes active participation in the learning process and involves self evaluation and feed back, it is expected that orientation of the university and college teachers through self-learning material would lead to better learning outcomes.

Another factor that seems to act in favour of self learning material is the autonomy that it offers to the learners in planning their learning activities. This factor is more important in the case of teachers who are adults and have many personal and family responsibilities besides their professional duties. Because of the rigidity that habits acquire at the time of adult-hood, many of the teachers would not like to be guided or governed by others as far as their own learning is concerned. For example, there may be teachers who would like to undertake self-study in a cosy-armed easy chair, say after dinner; there may be others who would find free time for self-studies in the early mornings; there may still be others who would do self-studies in the office-free periods and so on. This implies that teachers can learn effectively when they have freedom to plan their own study schedules and not compelled to attend a formal classroom teaching.

Since self-learning material provides autonomy and independence to the learners to go through it according to their own time and pace, and since it offers freedom of responsibility for regulating their own learning, it is therefore expected that self-learning strategy will prove to be more effective for the teachers than traditional classroom teaching. It is self-directed learning (Moore, 1977) that is important for teachers and not the traditional classroom teaching where they are directed to learn from persons they may not like to be directed.

Besides, the observations made in favour of self-learning material in this chapter also find support from the theoretical writings in the field of distance education. For example, the theory of autonomy and independence in adult learning propounded by Wedemeyer (1983), in the context of distance education, suggests that autonomous and independent learning through the self-learning material is effective because

(i) the normal process of teaching and learning is carried in writing,

(ii) the teaching is individualized and learning takes place through the learners' activity,

(iii) learning is made convenient for the learner in his own environment, and

(iv) the learner takes responsibility for his progress, with freedom to start, stop and pace himself at will.

SUGGESTIONS

From what is already known about the effectiveness of self-learning material and the observations made in this chapter the following are suggested which may be helpful in directing future thinking of the policy-makers involved in the orientation programmes through distance mode:

> The important suggestion for the practitioners and planners is that they must review their decisions regarding the further expansion and establishment of Academic Staff Colleges in the country and consider launching of programmes through distance mode.

- The use of distance mode for the orientation of the university and college teachers is also suggested because, in a country like ours with paucity of funds and resources, it is going to be an economically viable mode.

- Thus, if economy and efficiency in the orientation of the university and college teachers are desired to be achieved then the suggestion is significant as it has shown the way for a rethinking and re-consideration of the suggestions given by the Mehrotra Committee to launch professional orientation programmes of the teachers through the Indira Gandhi National Open University (IGNOU).

Besides this, launching of teacher education programmes at tertiary level through distance mode is also advocated because of the following benefits:

(i) It will result in the non-payment of TA/DA to the teachers while undergoing training.

(ii) It will not affect the regular teaching/learning process in the parent departments from where these teachers are deputed to be oriented as they can learn while working.

(iii) It will minimize the expenditure involved in the payment of TA/DA to the experts called for delivering lectures to the participants at the ASCs all over the country.

(iv) Heavy expenditure in establishing a number of ASCs all over the country will be saved as teachers can train themselves wherever they are according to their time, pace and capacity through self-learning materials.

(v) It will ensure the academic viability of teacher orientation because teachers would train themselves only when they are really motivated to learn at their will.

It is hoped that the arguments made in this chapter would help to identify if distance mode, i.e. teaching through self-learning materials could be effectively used for the orientation of university and college teachers. Such information could assist policy-planners and university administrators concerned with the professional orientation of university and college teachers to re-think and re-plan the strategies adopted for the orientation of the teachers at the tertiary level. This chapter, therefore, brings home the role of Indira Gandhi National Open University (IGNOU) to impart orientation programmes to teachers at the tertiary level by preparing pedagogically sound self-learning material on the content intended to be delivered to these teachers.

APPENDIX -I

LIST OF ASCs SELECTED IN THE SAMPLE

Sl. No	Name of ASCs	No. of Ops conducted	No. of participants	Area of Operation
1	2	3	4	5
1.	Guwahati University Ghy-14	31 (Upto March 1999)	1076	North-Eastern Region (10% from outside)
2.	Punjab University Chanigarh - 14	42(Upto March) 1999)	1236	Punjab, Haryana, Himachal Pradesh, and Jammu and Kashmir
3.	Himachal Pradesh University Shimla - 5	43(Upto March) 1999)	1035	Open
4.	University of Kashmir Srinagar - 6	25(Upto March) 1999)	396	Northern India
5.	University of Delhi Delhi	33(Upto March) 1999)	1004	North and Centre
6.	Gujarat University Ahmedabad - 9	19(Upto March) 1999)	656	Gujarat University, South Gujarat, University and S.P. University, Gujarat

1	2	3	4	5
7.	Utkal University Bhubaneswar	40(Upto March) 1999)	1183	Orissa, Eastern Region of India, Madhya Pradesh and Andhra Pradesh
8.	University of Mysore Mysore - 6	37(Upto March) 1999)	1141	Mysore, Banglore, Mangalore and Kuvempu University
9.	Madrass University	41 (Upto March) 1999)	1385	University of Madrass
10.	University of Calcutta Calcutta - 9	38(Upto March) 2000)	1257	West Bengle, 10% from other states, specially the sates of Eastern India
11.	Pune University Pune-7	81 (Upto March) 2000)	2786	Affiliated colleges of University of Pune, Shivaji University. North Maharastra
12.	University of Mumbai Mumbai	—	—	University. SNDT Women's University Tilak Maharastra Vidyapeeth, Deccan College and Bharati Vidyapeeth.

APPENDIX -II

1. ACADEMIC STAFF COLLEGE
UNIVERSITY OF MUMBAI
51st ORIENTATION PROGRAMME
(21.02.00 TO 23.03.00)

Component A : Awareness of linkages between Society, Environment, Development and Education

- Gandhi
- The teacher: Outside the Classroom
- Library
- Water situation in Maharastra (Environmental Issue for the 21st Century)
- Values and Ethics
- Slums in Mumbai
- Women Issues
- Secular Films

Component B : Philosophy of Education, Indian Education System and Pedagogy

- Teaching-learning Method
- Effective Lecturing
- University System
- University and Teachers' Problems

Component C : Subject Up gradation

- Participants' Presentation
- Remote Sensing

- Demonstration of audio-Visual Aids, Computer
- Book Review

Component D: Management and Personality Development

- Buzz Session
- Creative Skills
- Stress Management
- Symposia

2. ACADEMIC STAFF COLLEGE HIMACHAL PRADESH UNIVERSITY 1ST TO 37TH ORIENTATION PROGRAMME

Component A: General Awareness

- Indian Culture
- Economic Trends
- Public interest Litigation
- National Movement
- National Integration, Poverty and Unemployment
- Reservation Policy, Secularism
- Feminism
- University Autonomy
- Politicization of Crime in Education
- Tourism
- Himachal Culture Terrorism
- Communication
- Ecology and Society Corruption
- Journalism

- Social Change
- Yoga and Health
- Youth Power, Science and Technology, Scientific Temper
- College and UGC
- Modernization
- Indian Constitution, Consumerism
- Linguistic Problem and Social Change, International Politics
- Indian Economic Scene
- Remote Sensing
- Human Rights
- Population Education
- Literature and Life

Component B: Philosophy and Education

- Indian Education System and Pedagogy, Education System in India
- Objective of Education
- Problems and Issues in Higher Education, Role of a Teacher
- Measurement and Evaluation
- Learning Process, Communication
- Teaching
- Distance Education, Teachers Autonomy
- Personality Barriers to Learning
- Teaching Effectively, Adolescent Learning, Professionalisation of Teaching
- Educational Philosophy

- Report of Different Education Commissions
- Teaching Strategies at Tertiary Level of Education

Component C: Subject Up gradation

- Latest Conceptual Development in the Subject
- Scrutiny of Syllabi and Dividing them into Teachable Parts
- Methodology Issues in Study of the Subject
- Relevance of Curriculum in the Perspective of Social Aspirations and needs
- Effective Teaching, Techniques in the Concerned Subject
- The Issues for Research and Further Study
- Teaching Materials and Teaching Aids in the Subject

Component D: Management and Personality Development

- Teacher as a Leader, Campus Unrest
- Professional Ethics
- Socialization
- Management of Library Services
- Communication Skill
- Management of Examination System
- Classroom Management
- Interpersonal Effectiveness
- Stress Management
- Management of Education
- Effective Writing
- Public Speaking
- Group Dynamics

- Creativity
- Brain Storming
- Fishbowl technique
- Panel Discussion
- Group Discussion
- Debate
- Symposia
- Educational Planning
- Role Playing
- Conflict Management
- Making Arguments
- Comprehensive Skills

3. ACADEMIC STAFF COLLEGE UNIVERSITY OF MADRAS ORIENTATION COURSE, BATCH - XXXXI (FROM 01.03.1999 TO 28.03.1999)

Component A: Awareness of Linkages between Society, Environment, Development and Education

- Education for 2000
- Abuses among Students and Legal Perspectives
- Leadership Style
- Higher Education - Community Linkages
- Preparing Students for Secularism
- UGC and Professional Development Programmes
- Human Rights

- Gender Issues
- Environmental Education
- Challenges in Higher Education, Indian Education

Component B: Philosophy of Education, Indian Education System and Pedagogy

- National Policies on Education
- Classroom Learning and Educational Psychology
- Teaching and Learning Concepts
- Modified Lecture Method
- Adolescent Behaviour Curriculum Designing
- Teaching Skills
- Economics of Education and Privatization in Education
- Teaching Practice and Computer
- Information Technology Based Resources
- Workshop on Student Assessment
- Inter disciplinary Teaching
- Trends in Adult Education
- Guidance and Counseling
- Assertive Training
- Establishing Vocational Centres in Colleges

Component C: Subject Upgradation

- Research Design
- Workshop on Writing for Print Media
- Computer Instruction
- Research Proposal and Report Writing
- Panel Discussion

Component D: Management and Personality Development

- Self-Development through Simplified Kundalini Yoga
- Discipline Management
- Time Management
- Workshop on Public Speaking
- Organizing Conference, Seminars and Workshops
- Communication Skills
- Evolving Code of Conduct for Teachers
- Personality Development
- Faculty Development

4. ACADEMIC STAFF COLLEGE PUNJAB UNIVERSITY 37TH ORIENTATION PROGRAMME

Component A:

- Literacy Campaign
- Clash of Civilization: A New Western Missive
- People's Participation in Rural Development
- Art Appreciation
- Sahitya Kyon Padhen?
- Overuse of Synthetic Chemicals
- Liberalisation
- Emerging World Order
- Present Energy Scene
- Animal Diversity

- Journey Through Himalayas
- E-mail: What, Why and How
- Communalism

Component B:

- Information Processing Models in Curriculum Transaction
- Motivating the Learner
- Student Problems
- Learning for Teaching Effectively
- Teaching Games
- Computers Fundamentals
- Problems of Youth
- Good Writing is a Craft
- Develop your own Style of Teaching

Component C:

- Modalities of Teacher's Evaluation
- How to be a Better Teacher
- Use of Indicators in Research

Component D:

- Breaking the Ice
- Leadership Qualities in Teachers
- Thinking Creatively
- Making Arguments
- Stress Management

5. ACADEMIC STAFF COLLEGE GAUHATI UNIVERSITY ORIENTATION COURSE XXX (21.10.98 TO 08.09.98)

Component A: Awareness of Linkages between Society, Environment, Development and Education

- Understanding Human Culture
- Status of Women
- UGC and Financial Assistance to Higher Education
- Education as an Instrument of Development
- Socio-culture Perspectives of Development
- Science in Ancient India
- Environmental Education
- Social relations Among Communities
- Education and Human Value
- The Problems of Unemployment and Poverty in the North-East Region
- Secularism and National Integration
- The concept of Human Culture
- Environmental Pollution and Management
- Human Development and Poverty
- Literacy Mission and its Methodology with Reference to Assam
- Conservation of Nature
- Student Unrest: How to Tackle
- Women in Education, Indian Heritage
- Indian Culture and Modernization
- Scientific Temper

- Role of Teachers Beyond Classroom Teaching
- Population Education, Society in Assam
- Role of NGO in Socio-Economic Development

Component B: Philosophy of Education, Indian Education System and Pedagogy

- Problems of Teaching and Learning in College, including Role of Teachers in College Education
- Problems of Higher Education
- Computer Literacy and Internet
- History of Higher Education in India
- Teaching and Learning Problems of Higher Education
- Mental Health and College Students Counseling
- Adolescent Psychology
- Taxonomy of Educational Objectives
- College Governance
- Philosophy of Education
- Distance Education
- Library users Education, Study Skill, Self-Study, etc.
- Intelligence
- Affiliation and Management of College
- Motivation
- Reflections
- Vocational Education at First Degree Level
- Higher Education and its Maladies
- Psychology of Leaning
- Question Designing

- Micro-teaching
- Performance Appraisal and Teacher's Accountability

Component C: Subject Up gradation

- Research Methodology
- Practice Lecture
- Preparation of Project and Report Writing

Component D: Management and Personality Development

- Attributes of a Good Teacher
- Communication Skill
- Transaction Analysis
- Conflict Management
- Professional Development of Teachers
- Teachers and Teaching in India
- Management Function of Teachers, Teaching Effectiveness
- Critical Social Problems and Role of Teachers
- An Interaction Programme
- Teacher-administration Relationship

6. ACADEMIC STAFF COLLEGE
UNIVERSITY OF DELHI
ORIENTATION COURSE - XXXI

Component A: Awareness of Linkages between Society, Environment, Development and Education

- Introduction to the Course (OP)
- Education and Development

- Science, Scientific Values and Society
- Environment and Energy Scenario
- Job Oriented Courses: Future Perspective

Component B: Philosophy of Education, Indian Education system and Pedagogy

- Educational Planning in India
- Manpower Planning and Higher Education
- Higher Education and Transmission of Values
- Higher Education Scenario
- University Education; Problems of Students having Different School Background
- University Education, Problems of Rural-urban Dichotomy W.R.T. SC./ST. Students
- Integrated Approach to Students Development at University
- Imparting Knowledge - 'Lecture Methods'
- Imparting Knowledge - 'Interaction Method'
- Evaluation Process and Objective Item Test
- Use of Audio-Visual Aids
- Distance Mode in Higher Education
- Micro-teaching
- Examination System: Problems and Perspectives

Component C: Subject Up gradation

- Health care in India
- Research - a Second Dimension of University Education
- Planning for Teaching a Course
- Teaching and Research: Status and Suggestions for Improvement

Component D: Management and Personality Development

- Professional Development of Teacher - a Need of the Day
- Management of Higher Education - Role of EC.
- Management of University Academics - Role of AC.
- Management of Colleges - Role of Governing Bodies
- Management of Education - Role of Teacher Association
- Sports, Physical fitness and its Management at University Level
- What Does it Mean to Be a University Teacher
- Motivation of Teachers of Higher Education
- Functions of Teachers and their Professional and Career Development
- Students Unrest: Problem of Management

7. ACADEMIC STAFF COLLEGE UNIVERSITY OF MYSORE 37TH ORIENTATION PROGRAMME (31.05.99 TO 26.06.99)

Component A: Awareness of Linkages between Society, Environment, Development and Education

- Scientific Temper
- Human Rights Education
- Regionalism in India
- Social aspects of the Indian Constitution

- Economic Aspects of the Indian Constitution
- Relevance of Gandhism Today
- Economic Policy of India
- Challenge of Higher Education in the next Millennium
- Problems of Poverty in India
- India's Population Policy
- Democracy in India - Problems and Prospects
- Environment and Development
- Intellectual Property Right
- Dr. Ambedkar's Concept of Social Justice
- Economic Development Scenario in India
- AIDS Awareness
- Rural Development in India
- Plants and Environment Protection
- National Integration Secularism in India
- Urbanization in India - Problems and Management
- Indian Federalism and Centre-State Relations
- Social Tensions in India - Causes and Possible Remedies

Component B: Philosophy of Education, Indian Education System and Pedagogy

- Computer Education
- New Education Policy and Objectives
- Psychology of Education
- Objectives of Higher Education
- Values in Higher Education
- Creativity and Innovativeness in Higher Education

- Examination System and Reforms
- Psychology of Learning
- Philosophy and Objectives of Education
- Tutorial and Preparation for Teaching
- Health and Higher Education in India
- Internet
- New Teaching Methods
- Audio-Visual aids in Teaching
- Curriculum Design
- Computer Demonstration

Component C: Subject Up gradation

- Research methods in Higher Education
- Relevance of the 12th Century Kannada
- Kannada Language and Development
- Research Projects and Funding Agencies
- Subject Up gradation
- Consumer's Protection
- Recent Trend in Kannada
- Seminar on Commerce and Management
- Relevance of English Studies
- New Development in Modern Kannada Literature
- Seminar on Kannada
- Impact of Globalization in Indian Economy
- Seminar on Political Science
- Amartya Sen's Welfare Economics

Component D: Management and Personality Development

- Communication - Theory and Practice

- Understanding Self Stress Management
- Teaching Skills
- Models of Teaching
- Role and Responsibility of a Teacher
- Group Dynamic and Personality Development
- Counseling Students in Colleges
- Teacher as a Planner
- Evaluation of Teachers

8. ACADEMIC STAFF COLLEGE
GUJARAT UNIVERSITY
AHMEDABAD - 380009
18TH ORIENTATION COURSE
(15.07.98 TO 04.08.98)

Component A: Awareness of Linkages between Society, Environment, Development and Education

- Indian Tradition
- Remote Sensing
- Women and Society
- Economic Reforms
- Multiple Cultures
- Mass Communication Modernization
- Role of Academic Staff College (ASC)
- Population
- National Integration
- Consumer Education
- Pollution

- Pokhran Test
- Casteism
- Rural Development
- Secularism
- Technology and Society
- Integration

Component B: Philosophy of Education, Indian Education System and Pedagogy

- Non-formal Education
- Evaluation Methodology
- Competency in Education
- Education Models in West and India
- Distance Education
- Education System
- Computer Theory
- Philosophy of Education
- Value-based Education Motivation

Component C: Subject Up gradation

- Research Proposal

Component D: Management and Personality Development

- Role and Responsibilities of a Teacher
- Reference Skills
- Classroom Situation
- Effective Speaking
- Personality Development

9. ACADEMIC STAFF COLLEGE UNIVERSITY OF KASHMIR 21ST GENERAL ORIENTATION COURSE

Component A: Awareness of Linkages between Society, Environment, Development and Education

- Bio-diversity
- Atmospheric Pollution
- Education in Advanced Society
- Population Education
- Academic Staff College and its Relevance
- Role of Language in Society
- Delegation of Authority
- Law for the Layman
- Man and Environment
- Unbanisation

Component B: Philosophy of Education, Indian Education System Pedagogy

- Frustration
- Measurement
- Educational Technology
- Psychology of Teaching-learning Process
- Strategies in Higher Education
- Challenges in Higher Education
- Crisis in Higher Education
- Evaluation Patterns
- Motivation
- Creativity and Education

- Role of Authoritarian Education
- New Trends in Education
- Teaching in Higher Education
- Teacher and Higher Education
- Higher Education Policy and Perspective Use
- New Education Policy
- Re-emerging in Higher Education
- Higher Education and Grass Roots
- Grading System
- New Technology in Higher Education
- Distance mode of Education
- Evaluation in Higher Education
- Quality Control in Higher Education

Component C: Subject Up gradation

- Interest Rates and Liquidity Effects
- Concept of Teacher Education
- Research Quality and Quantity
- Institution of Deplaning Proceeding
- Research in Higher Education
- Seeking Procedures
- Concept of Distance Education

Bibliography

Abbot-Wood Report (1937) Ministry of Education, Government of India, New Delhi, Pp.24-27.

Ausubel, D.P. (1986) Educational Psychology: Cognitive View, Holt, Rinehart and Winston, New York.

Awang, A. (1981) 'Staff and Faculty Development in the Universities in Malaysia' in Staff and Faculty Development in Southeast Asia Universities, RIHED Research Series, Maruzen Investment, Hong Kong, p.53.

Bhusan, A. (1973) 'An Experimental Study of Linear Programme in Educational Statistics for B.Ed. Student -Teachers', Doctoral Dissertation, Meerut University, Meerut.

Chauhan, S.S. (1973) 'Developing a Programmed Text in Educational Psychology for B.Ed. Level', Doctoral Dissertation, Meerut University, Meerut.

Chalam, K. S. (1987) Academic Staff Orientation Scheme- Some Crucial Issues, University News, December, 14.

Das, B.C. (1990) 'Effectiveness of Self-learning Material for the Orientation of University and College Teachers', Doctoral Dissertation, Banaras Hindu University, Varanasi.

Dean, R.K. (1981) 'The Effectiveness of Study Guide Vrs. Programmed Instruction in Elastically Structured Teaching at West Virginia University'. Dissertation Abstract International, No.3, Vol.43, p. 1085-A.

Dhar, B. and Singh, T. (1990) Academic Staff College -A Developing Concept, Sterling Publishers Pvt. Ltd. Green Park Extension, New Delhi.

Despande, S. and Jantli, R.T. (1991) 'Effect of Orientation Course on Teaching Methods in Higher Education on the Attitude of Academic Staff College Participants towards Teaching at the Tertiary Level', University News, 29, 43,8-11, Oct 28.

Dilman, D.A. (1987) Response to Mail Survey: What We Know, What we do not know and what we need to find out? Paper read at ZUMA-Konferenz Zur Schriftlichen Befragungund Telefonischen Befragungsmethode, Mannheim: ZUMA, April 17- 30.

Dutta, J. (2000) Academic Staff Colleges as Nodal Centers for Excellence, University News, Vol.38 (1), AIU, New Delhi.

Edelman, U. (1983) 'Individualised Instruction in Mathematics and its Effect on Males and Females with Academic Disabilities', Dissertation Abstract International, No.1, Vol.44, P19-A.

Educational Policy (1904), Ministry of Education, Government of India, Delhi.

Educational Policy (1913), Ministry of Education, Government of India, Delhi.

Govinda, R. (1976) 'Development of a Programmed Text on Educational Evaluation and Experimentally Studying its Effectiveness as Instructional Material', in Second Survey of Research in Education, Buch, M, B. (1979), SERD, Baroda.

Grant, J.M. (1983) 'The Study of an Individualised Mode of Learning: A Comparison of Contrasting Methods in the Teaching of Freshman College Biology', Dissertation Abstract International, No.3, Vol. 44, P-682-A.

Hawes, G.R. and Lynne, S.H. (1982). The Concise Dictionary of Education, Van Nostrand Reinhold Co. New York, p.3.

Holmberg, B. (1973) 'The Swedish Delta Project: A Case Study' in Handle et al., The Selection of Relevant Media/ Methods for defined Educational Purposes within Distance Education, EHSC, Oslo.

Joshi, D.C. and Singh, S. (1978) 'Orientation Course for University Lecturers', Higher Education Monograph, No.4, Case, M.S. University, Baroda.

Joseph, A. (1993) Academic Staff College: The Need for a New Model. University News, January, 11, Vol.XXXI, P.11.

Johnston, J.M.and Pennypecker, H.S. (1977) Behavioural Approach to College Teaching, American Psychologist. No26, pp 219-244.

Kapur, J.N. (1992) Academic Staff College Refresher Courses Curricular Changes. University News, Vol. XXX, April 30.

Kasinath, H.M. and Patel, G.M. (1995) Pre - induction Training Course to Improve Teaching in Higher Education. University News 33(2), January, 9, pp.11-14.

Knowles, A. S. (Editor-in Chief, 1977). The International Encyclopedia of Higher Education, Jossey-Bass Publishers, San Francisco, p. 1613.

Koul, L.(1988) Methodology of Educational Research, Vikash Publishing House Pvt. Ltd. New Delhi.

Lee, M.M. and Mclean, J.E. (1978) 'A Comparison of Achievement and Attitude among Three Methods of Teaching Educational Psychology', The Journal of Educational Research, No.2, Vol. 72, pp86-89.

Mehrotra, R.C. (1993) 'Professional Development of Teachers: Orientation Programmes and Refresher Courses', University News, Vol. 30(1), AIU, New Delhi.

Moonis, R. and Sharma, G.D. (1986) Professional Development of Teachers, Report by , the Study Group for National Commission on Teachers in Higher Education (1983-85), NIEPA, New Delhi.

Moore, M.G. (1977) On a Theory of Independence Study, Fern Universitat, Hagen.

Mullick, S.P.(1964) 'An Experiment on a Programmed Learning Lesson in a Correspondence Course', in a Survey of Research in Education, Buch, M.B. Baroda, CASE, 1974.

National Policy on Education (1986) Ministry of Human Resource Development, Government of India, New Delhi.

Neuberger, G.B. (1984) 'The Effect of Individualised Instruction Programme on Education of Outpatients with Rheumatoid Arthritis,' Dissertation Abstract International, No. I, Vol.44, P.3271-A.

Otto, S.G.Z. (1981) 'The Effect of Individualised Instruction in Physical Education on Student Teachers and their Students', Dissertation Abstracts, International, No. 1, Vol.42,p.132-A.

Pandey, S.N. (1981) 'Effectiveness of Different Strategies used for Teaching B.Ed. Students', Unpublished Dissertation, Banaras Hindu University, Varanasi.

Pandey, S. (1990) Teachers for the Twenty First Century: Redefining Professionalism for Global Perspective, University News, Vol.36 (6), Feb.9, AIU, New Delhi.

Passi, B.K. and Pal, R. (1991) Academic Staff Colleges: The Relevance of Their Curricula, New Frontiers in Education, 21, 3, July-Sept.

Passi, B.K. and Pal, R. (1992) Resource Persons of the Academic Staff College, New Frontiers in Education, 22,3, July-Sept.

Patil, D. (1995) Academic Staff College: Achievements and Constraints in Implementation of Higher Education Policy- A Review. Higher Education Unit, NIEPA, 17 B. Sri Aurobindo Marg, New Delhi.

Programme of Action, NPE (1986) Government of India, New Delhi.

Rao, P.H.S. and Palsane M.N. (1994) Training for Higher Education, Rawat Publications, Jaipur.

Rao, S. (1993) Some Thoughts on Planning in Higher Education, University News, Vol.3, March, 8.

Rastogi, S. (1998) Academic Staff Development in Higher Education, University News, Vol.36, August 17.

Rehman and Biswal (1992) How Effective are Orientation Programmes of the Academic Staff Colleges: Analysis of Participants Evaluation, University News, 30(13) March 30.

Report of the Education Commission (1964-66), Ministry of Education, Government of India, PP. 155-525.

Report of the Secondary Education Commission (1952-53), Ministry of Education, Government of India, New Delhi.

Report of the University Education Commission (1948-49), Ministry of Education, Government of India, New Delhi.

Report of the Indian Education Commission (1882) Government of India, Delhi.

Report of National Commissions on Teachers (1983-85), Government of India, New Delhi.

Report of Mehrotra Committee (1986), Ministry of Human Resource Development, Government of India, New Delhi.

Report of the Sargent Commission (1944) Ministry of Education, Government of India, Delhi.

Rosovsky, H. (1994) Indian Education System: Revitalization and Reform in Mathur, M.V. (Ed.) Willey Eastern, New Delhi.

Rothkopf, E.Z.(1996) 'Learning from Written Instructive Material: An Exploration of the Control of Inspection Behaviour by Test-like Events', American Educational Research Journal, Vol. 1, No. 3, New York.

Sansanwal, D.N. (1978) 'An Experimental Study in Programmed Learning for Teaching Research Methodology Course at the M.Ed. Level', in

Second Survey of Research in Education, Buch, M.B., Baroda, SERD, 1979.

Shah, I.K. (1980) 'Developing a Teaching Strategy for the Course on Educational Evaluation at the M.Ed. Level and Studying its Effectiveness',' Doctoral Dissertation, M.S. University, Baroda.

Sheppard, W.C. (1970) Design and Evaluation of a Programmed Course in Introductory Psychology, Journal of Applied Behaviour Analysis, No.1, Vol.3, PP.5-11.

Singh, G. (1997) Academic Staff College: An Assessment, University News, 35, (14), April 7.

Singh, D. (1989) 'Developing Self learning Material and Trying out its Efficacy for Teaching Techniques of Teaching to B.Ed. Students', Doctoral Dissertation, B.H.U., Varanasi.

UNESCO, Roadmap (1986) Academic Staff Development -Higher Education, UNESCO, Bankok.

Vatabavigkit, S. (1985) 'A Personalized System of Instruction in Mathematics for Thai College Students', Dissertation Abstract International, No.2, Vol.46, P.370-A.

Vijaykumar. K.C. (1998) Revamping Refresher Courses, University News, Vol.36, No. 41, Oct, 12.

Wedemeyer, C.A. (1983) Six Distance Education Theorists, ZIFF: Hagen

Woods Despatch (1854) Government of India, Delhi.

Yadav, M.S. and Roy, S. (1977) Professional Orientation for University Teachers- A Programme, Educational Trends, 12, pp. 1-3.

INDEX